What The F[uck] Is A "Spiritual Awa[kening]" Anyway?

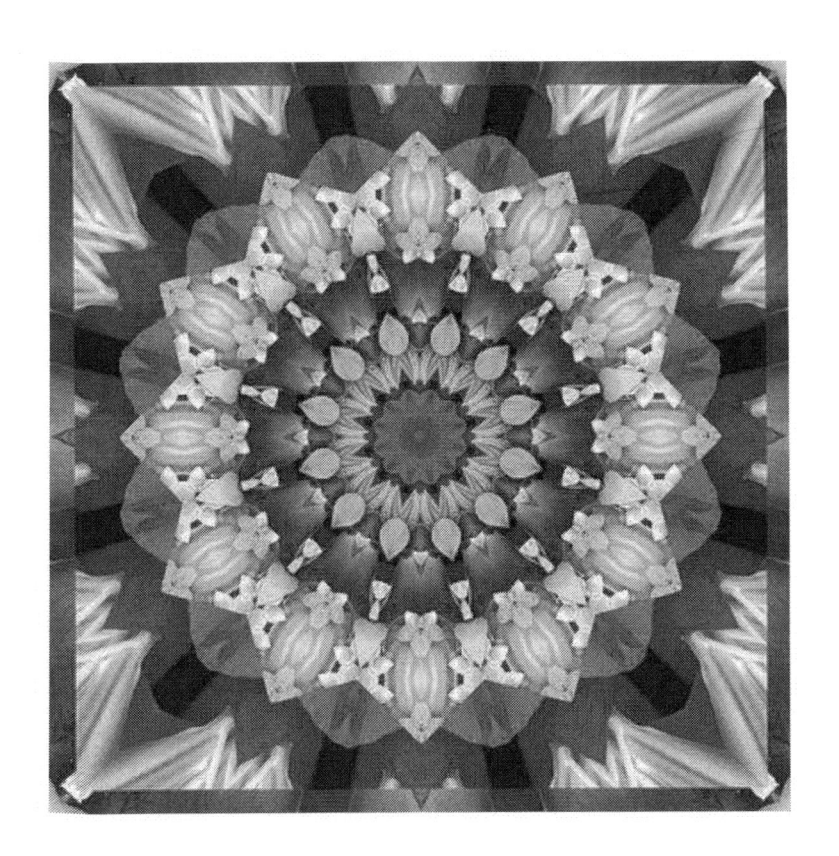

By
Emma Lucy Wall
© Emma Lucy Wall 2021

Terms and Conditions

LEGAL NOTICE

© Copyright 2021 **Emma Lucy Wall**

All rights reserved. The content contained within this book may not be reproduced, duplicated, or transmitted without direct written permission from the author or the publisher. Email requests to kevin@babystepspublishing.com

Under no circumstances will any blame or legal responsibility be held against the publisher, or author, for any damages, reparation, or monetary loss due to the information contained within this book, either directly or indirectly.

Legal Notice:

This book is copyright protected. It is only for personal use. You cannot amend, distribute, sell, use, quote or paraphrase any part, or the content within this book, without the consent of the author or publisher.

Disclaimer Notice:

Please note the information contained within this document is for educational and entertainment purposes only. All effort has been executed to present accurate, up to date, reliable, complete information. No warranties of any kind are declared or implied. Readers acknowledge the author is not engaging in the rendering of legal, financial, medical, or professional advice. The content within this book has been derived from various sources. Please consult a licensed professional before attempting any techniques outlined in this book.

By reading this document, the reader agrees under no circumstances is the author responsible for any losses, direct or indirect, that are incurred as a result of the use of the information contained within this document, including, but not limited to, errors, omissions, or inaccuracies.

Published by Babysteps Publishing Limited

https://babystepspublishing.com

All enquires to kevin@babystepspublishing.com

The image on the front cover is created by David Sun Todd. This image is named Infinity. David's work is available as wall art, on home furnishings, lifestyle items and clothing.

You can see more of David's beautiful creations from his website. https://bellandtodd.pixels.com/art

Table of Contents

Why I Wrote This Book? 1
Why Should You Read This Book? 5
Chapter 1 Downloads 11
Chapter 2 Higher Selves 23
Chapter 3 Guides 29
Chapter 4 Everyone Can Do This 33
Chapter 5 Paradigms 39
Chapter 6 Meditation 43
Chapter 7 How To Meditate 53
Chapter 8 Can Anybody Do This? 57
Chapter 9 Shifting Consciousness 63
Chapter 10 Abundance and Manifestation 67
Chapter 11 Spirituality and Money 73
Chapter 12 Going Forward 79
About the Author 81
Other Books and Services by the Author 83
One More Thing Before You Go… 85

Why I Wrote This Book?

I wrote this book to help people. I wrote this book to demystify some of the language around Spirituality. I wrote this book because I am an ordinary woman who is having some very extraordinary experiences (finally) and I know you can have them too.

I also wrote the book because I was told to. I was told to. By God, the Universe, Source, Spirit. I call it GUSS for short. I saw two psychics over six months, and they both told me that I needed to write this book.

So here I am writing this book.

I'm also writing this book because I've long since had the feeling that when it is on the number one bestsellers list, it will be an absolute demonstration that this stuff works. I have been manifesting it for years.

A few years ago, having brought my children up for 18 years, I had to go back to work. I had to go back to a corporate job and I pitched myself as low as I could possibly go.

It was really quite depressing. I walked into the office one day in May 2018, and I just felt my heart fall out of me. I didn't really want to be there. It felt like a graveyard. The people, I have to say, were lovely but I felt like I was in some kind of a cage and I've always been such a free spirit. I really could not bear to be where I was so I began a journey of escape.

My name is Emma Lucy Wall and in December 2020 I took the biggest leap of faith in my life. I surrendered myself entirely to the Universe to see what would unfold. In this book, I'm going to tell you what did unfold, and how you can do the same. I'm going to tell you the secret, the magic, that the whole lot is available to every man, woman and child on this planet. You just need to believe, take action, surrender, and watch the magic happen.

Okay so let's back up a little. If you'll indulge me. Let me tell you a little bit about myself.

I was born in 196something or other to loving parents and three big brothers. I was the much-longed-for first girl and, although my brothers loved me, we were already quite a crowd. I believe there was some jealousy and hostility towards me. My dad moved a lot with his job and my mum was at home alone with four children under five followed not long after by another little boy and finally another girl. So, then we were six.

We had an ordinary upbringing on the whole. Our parents loved us. We were safe. We had everything we needed although we were very aware that "money doesn't grow on trees", and our mother "didn't have a bottomless purse, you know". We lived briefly in Germany where my dad was working, and we had some adventures there.

Shortly after we returned from Germany, my parents relocated again, and finally, to North London.

We left a very well to do town in Buckinghamshire in the South East of England. I was seven years old and, as I write this, I know that that was where the trouble in my life started.

The house we were moving into was a wonderful three-storey Victorian building. It had enormous potential but when my parents bought it, the house was divided up into bedsits that needed to be ripped out and the house put back together. At the time it was completely uninhabitable.

We had to live in a tiny flat up the road for what my parents assure me was only a couple of weeks, but to my seven-year-old self, it felt like six months. There was frost on the inside of the windows and damp and mould everywhere. It smelt really bad. I felt very unsafe. Plus the house my parents had bought was a building site. It seemed to cause a lot of upset, especially to my poor dad who was working full time and renovating a six-bedroom house at the weekends. I remember it feeling a bit like painting the Forth Bridge - the renovation was never-ending. It never got to feel complete.

That's not to say that I was unhappy or that the family was unhappy. It was just a very far cry from Wendover, Buckinghamshire where we had been before. Plus, we had to reinvent ourselves. We were posh, and we had landed in North London. I remember a family friend giving us inverse elocution lessons, how to drop T's and flatten our vowels so that we would fit in and not get beaten up. I guess that is where a sense of lack came in.

We had left our beautiful warm comfortable home and had moved into a building site with draughty windows and a slightly hostile daily environment.

I had a healing session recently where the healer found my seven-year-old self. Apparently, she gave up on wants and desires around about then.

Now, none of this is bad. I was still safe. People have much worse upbringings than mine, but this is a book about spiritual awakening, and in order to understand how I woke up, it helps to understand how and why I went to sleep.

Why Should You Read This Book?

You should read this book because my life is a demonstration of deliberate creation (and not so deliberate creation). My experiences, my choices, my decisions, just like yours, are what shaped and created my reality.

You should read this book because I ground the spiritual into the physical. I take the mumbo jumbo out of the spiritual vocabulary. And I use my own life experiences to demonstrate the spiritual path.

I didn't have a big bells and whistles moment of enlightenment. I didn't see angels dancing around my bedroom. I wasn't gifted an incredible life-changing insight or code. I have just put one foot in front of the other, followed the Universe's breadcrumbs and have arrived today in your living room (or wherever you are) where I will share the wisdom, the lessons and the insights I have gleaned into how this game of life actually works.

When I was seven, my little (or big) soul, which had come down to have this amazing abundant experience was most certainly not having that experience. I did not feel that I had reached the Promised Land and not long after, my pubescent brothers began to turn on me

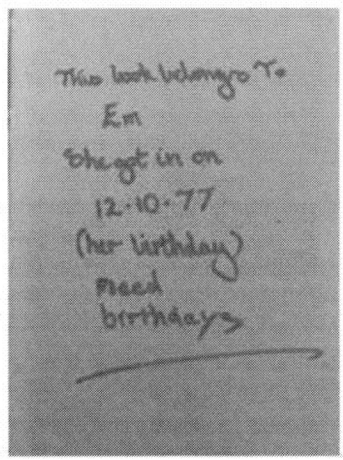

On my 10th birthday, I was given the same cookery book twice. I still have one copy, and there's an inscription in it.

Oh, dear. Can you feel how the bitterness and the ingratitude were getting stuck in? Self-pity was taking root in my soul and I was on my way to a long and self-perpetuating relationship with victim energy.

I'm not sure exactly what was going on in my parents' marriage at this stage, but I do know that my mum's mum, our beloved granny, became extremely ill with pancreatic cancer and died very soon after her diagnosis. My grandfather spiralled quickly into dementia after granny died and to top it off, my mum's sister Katie, (a princess like me), was diagnosed with breast cancer two years after their mother died. She battled that cancer for 10 years until she finally slipped away - her children aged 24, 22 and 18.

Meanwhile, I was in and out of the hospital with Quinsy and endless tonsillitis, which culminated in a tonsillectomy when I was around 13. My poor mother. As I write this, I feel for her. I'm a mother of three now and my five siblings are all still well and both of my parents are alive and kicking.

Fast forward to 15-year-old Emma. I'm profoundly and completely in love with my first boyfriend, Rob. He was so cool. I fancied all my brother's friends one by one and in the end, I snagged the best one. He was super cool, super sexy, and we adored each other.

I spent every hour I could at Rob's house. He lived just around the corner from me, and we spent hours making out, smoking pot and talking and talking and talking about everything. I was so blessed to have this older man in my life, teaching me so much. It was fun. I was happy. Reflecting back, I can see that Rob was probably my first spiritual teacher.

I haven't mentioned Catholicism yet, have I?

Catholicism really didn't resonate with me. I found the energy around churches dark and unwelcoming. I had no idea why, but I hated mass. I made my first Holy Communion casually at a house mass. Thank God I got away without having to do the whole bride of Christ thing that First Holy Communion makes me think of.

I remember going to confession, aged around 11 and thinking, "but I haven't done anything wrong". I made up some nonsense about not always being kind to others. I don't think I had been unkind until then, but the week after the confession I pushed a pretty girl in my year down the stairs at school. I got in terrible trouble for that and I never went to Confession again. I declined Confirmation as I knew that would be me consciously taking on the edicts of the Catholic Church, and that was not about to happen.

By now, manifestation was beginning to creep in. Of course, it was always there but I had no idea I was manifesting. Looking back now I realise that I was actually manifesting a lot of misery - by feeling sorry for myself.

I did manifest Rob – yay - and about halfway through my first O level year, my aged biology teacher retired. She told us that her replacement was tall, dark and handsome. My ears pricked up. I had always favoured the older gentleman and liked to have a teacher crush going on most of the time.

He started after the Easter holidays. Oh my god. I still remember him walking in. Tall - check, he was six foot one. Dark - check, and incredibly handsome. He reminded me of Clark Kent. I was in heaven. I had three years of this Adonis ahead of me. I used to sit at the back of the class just gazing at him. My heart would beat faster in practical lessons when he'd cruise the room and come and check our work. I was completely smitten. In fact, I would lie in bed at night, imagining scenes that are way too blue for this book.

I was still with Rob at this time and Mr T was happily married with his first two children being born during the time he taught me. It was just a harmless fantasy, right? Watch this space …

Years passed. My A levels didn't go so well. I took a job as a lab technician at what was at that time Glaxo Group Research Limited. My plan was to work my way up through the ranks and be sponsored to study pharmacy.

Luckily, my dad intervened. I was miserable. My relationship with Rob was petering out. My friends had all gone away to university and were having a ball and I was getting up at 6 am, and sitting in Rob's car as he raced impatiently across London. I knew this wasn't my life.

My dad persuaded me to leave the job and go back to college and get my degree. I did but I wasn't very engaged and I befriended a 50-year-old gay man and a couple of people in their 20s who were safely in relationships. I knew if I hung out with people in my own age group, my relationship with Rob would not stand a chance. In fact, my relationship with Rob didn't stand a chance. We split up halfway through my second year. It was very painful. Seven years together took a lot of unpicking.

So now, here I was - a 21-year-old lost in the world, but a survivor. I finished my degree, tried to go around the world, didn't actually get very far. I spent a long hot summer in France getting brown and chubby. I came home and tried Manchester. I came home after six months when the pain in my chest became insufferable. The day I left for good that pain lifted. It's incredible what the body knows.

Back in the South East of England, I began catering. Yay. I was home. One of my first homes. I loved my work and I immersed myself in it completely. I did a post-graduate professional qualification in hotel and catering management and I had a lot of fun.

One of the guys on the course (Andy) turned out to be the best friend of one of Mr T's closest friends. Andy kindly shared with me that Mr T was now divorced, and he also took the precaution of telling his mate that I was now a fully grown, sexually active woman.

At the same time [I love the Universe] Mr T met my mother at a blood donating session. They chatted and he asked after me. She told him I was in catering and he happened to be responsible for organising the catering for the staff of the school.

It's FA Cup Final day 1995. I've just spent a few weeks living with my mum between homes and was popping into town to buy her a box of chocolates to say thank you when who should come cycling around the corner, but Mr T himself. He stopped. We chatted. It was a bit weird and slightly charged.

The next day, I was packing up to move into my new home and there was a knock at the door. It was Mr T. He wanted to know about catering. I promised him I would send him some information and then I ran upstairs and called my best friend. She hooted with laughter and sang, "You're gonna bag the teacher". A couple of faltering steps later, I did indeed "bag the teacher".

Three years later and 15 years after I first set eyes on him [and with no laws broken or relationships compromised], Mr T and I married. We spent the next 15 years together. Now that's manifestation.
Along the way, I manifested other things. Pregnant with my first child, I read a book about pregnancy and childbirth. There was a chapter in the book about stillbirth. The author was insistent that I read the chapter so that I would be prepared if such a tragedy were to befall me.

Five years later, on the day my firstborn was first diagnosed with Attention Deficit Disorder, my third child, our only son, stopped moving in my belly. His light went out and he was surgically removed from my belly four days later. Our baby boy. JJ - Joseph John touched our lives and the lives of those around us so deeply. 17 years later. As I write this, I'm grateful for the learning, the enrichment of my family and my consciousness of that experience.

Wow, this is beginning to sound like a great long tale of woe. And in fact, I do believe that it is from suffering and pain that we learn our greatest lessons. Most people, in my experience, who find themselves on a spiritual path have known intense pain in the physical realm. And as you'll hear later, I believe this is part of the soul's journey. It's the suffering that leads to the existential crisis, out of which growth will come when we let it.

It was becoming apparent that our firstborn was not neurotypical. My ex-husband was a mainstream teacher and we knew that mainstream school was not a good environment for her. So, we moved.

We left our supportive community in North London, which had been our home, between us, for 64 years. We moved to Hertfordshire, in order that our oldest daughter could go to a Steiner School.

This was a shock to our systems. Not only were we dealing with leaving our community but my mother-in-law was dying. Our second daughter was wrenched from a school and home where she was perfectly happy, and we now had a one-year-old baby.

The Steiner School and the people it attracted were completely out of our comfort zone. I remember going to a class picnic and a Colombian woman dive-bombing me about Angelic Reiki. Angelic what ?!?!? This was all completely alien to me.

We went on a group skiing trip. My oldest and my youngest couldn't ski, so I ended up in the chalet, with a woman who astral travelled and communed with angels by day and went lucid dreaming by night. These dreams took her to past lives, and she spoke to me of aliens and telepathy.

There was colour therapy, aura transformation, statues of Buddha, crystals, sprouting wheat, chakras, and a lot of very strange smells. I was very confused, not sure what was going on or if I would ever understand but I'm a brave and fearless soul so I persevered.

Our marriage was spiralling downhill, and we were still grieving our son, my mother-in-law, our life in London, and now we had a diagnosis for our oldest - Autistic Spectrum Condition, Attention Deficit Disorder, Dyspraxia, Dyslexia and Dyscalculia. We couldn't find a home to buy. We had one foot in the mainstream and one in Steiner. We were an anomaly.

We had money though. Mr T's mother left a considerable sum and we used it for counselling and healing. I remember one healing, where I literally felt JJ's soul leave my aura and I began to understand what was going on.

I am telling you my life story to show you that I was not always "spiritually awake". I did a fair amount of suffering and spent a long time stumbling unconsciously through my life.

Many people do stumble unconsciously through life. In the western world, we don't have much help to do it any other way.

There is, right now, a great awakening or remembering or both across the planet and it is my wish that my experiences will resonate for you to a greater or lesser extent.

I send this book out as an offer of support and guidance to you as you begin to explore what these times might mean in your life.

Chapter 1
Downloads

I have a beautiful friend who is reluctantly living in New York City, locked down since COVID hit.

We met on a retreat in Bosnia and again, two weeks later in the Dorset/Devon borders of the UK. She is deeply spiritual - what might be described as 5th dimensional. She has a gentle flow about her, infinite wisdom. We often laugh together about downloads. Neither of us has ever consciously had what might be described as a "download". We don't see lights flashing. We don't hear voices in our heads or smell weird inappropriate smells, or taste curry at odd times of the day. We don't have premonitions and neither of us has knowingly met any ghosts. We do, however, both have what might be described as inner knowing. Things just feel right - or wrong.

Arguably, we're getting mini downloads all the time.

I knew, for example, when the publisher of this book crossed my path that he was the person I needed to work with in order to get the book into the world. And he knew it too.

Before I sat down to write it, and especially this chapter, I invited a download.

Whenever I connect with my guides, or my higher self, (which we'll talk about in later chapters), I feel their presence in my forearms. I had no idea why this was and I assumed it was to do with carrying some kind of weight around the world. Until I was told by another of my spiritual friends, that it is GUSS - God, the Universe, Source, Spirit - trying to come through me. My friend told me I needed to write a book.

Receiving a download is about trust and belief. Many aspects of spiritual awakening are ethereal and nebulous. They don't feel grounded. Only about 10% of the world's population is currently (April 2021 as I write) on this path. The spiritual experiences people are having are not those of the everyday.

One intuitive I am particularly fond of receives messages from a collection of guides he calls the Zees. For a long time, I found it hard to access that language. It all just sounded a bit silly.

And it is very alien to our way of being. I pick up a stone and I give it to you and you have no doubt that you have a stone in your hand. You can see it. You can feel it, smell it, taste it (if you want to), hear it (though it probably won't say much). But, when we're dealing with the energetic and spiritual worlds, we have very little physical evidence to offer. It's a big leap of faith to open ourselves to these possibilities and alternatives and our attachment to our physical experience can often keep the mind closed.

And yet ...

When I split up with my husband, I had a couple of really quite toxic relationships - one with a married man, (I'm sorry D) and one with a man who managed to destroy me completely in three months of texting abusively and amusingly, by turns. It was awful. I was a shell of myself and I had to do something. A good friend insisted that I go and have a massage. I decided to have a four-handed Lomi Lomi massage from a couple in the village I live close to.

Talk of a four-handed massage tends to raise the odd eyebrow, I'm sure you can imagine. But there was nothing sexual or kinky about this massage. It was among the most tender and loving experiences I've ever had in my adult life.

That couple held me and loved me like I was their child. I remember one of them cradling my head while the other stroked my hair and when they massaged the back of my heart space, my body rucked from the sobbing. This lovely couple were undoubtedly downloading something. They begin their beautiful massages by inviting "loving presence" into the space. And I did feel loved. I felt them completely present to me and to each other.

This was another wake-up call for me. The tenderness, the intuitive touch, the kindness, the love. This was more than just a massage. This was the channelling of energy through the medium of touch.

A few months later, I was chatting to my sister-in-law. I have no idea what I said which prompted her to say "you should try Kundalini Yoga". These days I would correct her and say I *could* try Kundalini Yoga.
"Kunda what?" I asked her.

"Kundalini Yoga," she said again. "Try it. I think you will love it".

By now, I was very much on a path to healing myself. The massage couple had put me onto Bach's flower remedies and invited me to an event at which we set our Life Compass. A few of us spent a Saturday afternoon in January drinking herbal tea and listening to soft music, in each other's loving presence. In that soft, nurturing space, we set our intentions for the coming year.

At that same event, I met another angel of a woman who introduced me to five rhythms, dancing, and a book called Playing Big by Tara Mohr.

I was open and curious. I wanted my life to be different. No more dodgy men. No more feeling like a victim. No more sleepwalking through life. So, I tracked down a Kundalini Yoga class near me, and I went. It was my second home coming. I have practised yoga since I was 17 but this … this did something to me, something deep inside. [Thank you, Paul Weller, for the lyrics].

This opened me up to a world I could not see. I can't pick up Kundalini energy and give it to you any more than I can pick up gravity and give it to you. But just as gravity keeps me from floating off into the atmosphere, Kundalini energy raised something in me. I became aware of the energy within me, outside me and all around me.

And from those first few classes, my entire business has grown and morphed and evolved.

I have continued to follow the nudges and suggestions from the Universe, and the more I follow them, the more my physical experience expands.

So back to downloads …

Life is full of twists and turns. At any given moment, we can choose this path or that path. We can ask questions of the Universe, and we can choose which direction to go in. Each choice will result in a different outcome.

I'm going to invite you at this point to stop reading. If you have 30 minutes right now. Give yourself a gift and go and meet your future self. https://healingmoney.kartra.com/page/futureself

I originally heard this meditation in Tara Mohr's book Playing Big, and she borrowed it from The Coaches Training Institute.

I created a beautiful version of this future self visualisation with a man who passed through my life from December 2019 to October 2020. It is my voice reading the words from the Coaches Training Institute, and John Christopher Scott added the music of Brahms.

You can also make your own recording if you prefer to listen to your voice or have somebody you love read the following to you.

The reason I invite you to do this visualisation is to get you to have an experience of energy.

Energy has no ties to time or space. It's going on all the time, in all of space.

In meeting your future self, you will find you're better able to discover where the resonances are for you. And that is where downloads come in.

Make sure you journal after the meditation. You will want to remember what you saw and experienced. This process will provide a set point for you to make all your life decisions from going forward.

After I wrote that last paragraph, I had an impulse to go and read about my future self journaling. I did the exercise over five years ago and, although I haven't quite made it to my beachside dwelling, I can honestly say that I live and make choices according to what I saw that day back in March 2016.

Now sit back, relax and tune in to your future self.

This is a meditation during which you will meet your future self. Your future self could also read your higher self. It's that part of you that you can reach out to for guidance at any moment when you're at a crossroads when you need help making a decision. Once you've met your future self, your higher self, it's so much easier to connect with them and to tune in to your most fundamental needs. This particular meditation is also recorded by a wonderful teacher called Tara Mohr. And she took it from the Coaches Training Institute. You can listen to Tara's version if you prefer. She's North American. If you prefer an English accent, then you've come to the right place.

So, find yourself a comfortable spot, a place where you can sit, a comfy chair or a sofa or you can recline in bed. Make sure you have a pen and a paper nearby as you're going to be invited at the end of the visualisation to write down some notes. Make sure you're going to be warm. You might want to have a blanket. It's best not to fall asleep if you can help it.

When you're ready, just relax. Close your eyes. Take some deep breaths down into your belly. Allow the muscles of the belly to relax completely. Begin breathing as if you were a little baby. Just softly breathing. As you breathe in, your belly distends and as you breathe out it drops back towards the spine. Relax the muscles around your eyes. Relax your jaw and let your cheeks feel heavy. Notice your breath as you inhale and exhale. Feel the cool air moving past your nostrils. As you come into this relaxed state, begin to imagine that your body is a body of water. A calm lake. As you take a breath in, notice the soft current in that body of water. And as you exhale, release some more tension and release any stress away from your body. Let any stress and any tension float away in the ripples of the water.

Now bring your attention down to your feet. Notice if you're carrying any tightness or stress in your feet. If you are, just soften there and let it go. Let a soft heaviness come into your feet. Move your attention to your calves and your shins and relax them. You can send your breath down there to loosen up the muscles. Soften the muscles around your knees. Breathe in and out and relax more deeply. Keep moving your attention upwards. Release your quads and your upper legs. Imagine any tension that's there just seeping away. As you take your next inhale imagine your breath moving into your hips, into your pelvic area and allow all those muscles to open up. As you exhale, let any stress and tension just melt away from the muscles in your hips and your pelvic bone. Let your belly fully release. Relax your torso. Relax your chest. Let any stress seep away from your back your lower back, your middle back, and your upper back.

Bring your attention to your shoulders. Let any tension there melt off down your back. Let it soften your shoulders across your collarbones. Relax the back of your neck, the front of your neck and your jaw.

Relax your tongue and your cheeks. Relax your temples, your eyes, your forehead and your scalp. Relax your arms, your upper arms, your elbows, forearms, your wrists, your hands and your fingers.

Now bring your attention to the spot on your forehead between your eyebrows - your third eye. Imagine a beam of light stretching out from your third eye. Take note of that beam of light. What colour is it? Is it sharp and precise? Or does it have blurred edges? Notice the quality. See how that beam of light stretches all the way up out of the room that you're in, above and through the ceiling above you and out through the roof of the building you're in. That beam of light shines out into the sky. Give yourself permission to travel along this beam of light. Imagine that you're floating up and walking along the beam of light out of the room where you are. You're following that beam upwards. Allow the beam to take you higher and higher. And as you look down you can see the building where you are getting smaller and smaller in your view. As you travel, notice the beauty of the sky and move through the clouds. Start to see the view of the city or the town that you were in below you. As you start to travel faster and higher, you can see the whole region where you were beneath you. Move up and up until you can see the globe, the beautiful globe of blue, and green, and white. Enjoy that view. Enjoy looking at our beautiful plant and keep travelling up and up until you're in blue-black space, where it's silent, velvety, and dark.

When you're there, notice that there's another beam of light running right next to the beam of light that you're on. Notice the colour and quality of that beam and notice that that beam stretches all the way back down towards Earth. That beam stretches down towards Earth 20 years from now, 20 years into the future.

Now, step off the beam that you're on onto that new beam and let it gracefully carry you down. Notice how the earth starts to come back into focus. The contours are getting clearer and larger in your view. Enjoy passing back through the clouds again as you make your way down. And as you begin to get close to Earth, start to notice that you're going home. But you're going to the home of your future self. You're going to the home of yourself 20 years from now. Notice that the beam is taking you to meet your future self.

What part of the world are you in? Continue riding that beam down. Enjoy the views below. You follow it all the way until it takes you to the home of your future self and drops you off. Right there. Before you approach the house itself, take a look around - What kind of a place is this? What's it like? What does it feel like?

Look around the outside of your future self's home. And then notice the house, the dwelling place. Make your way towards the door. Take in that home? What does it look like? What does it feel like?

As you approach the door, become aware of your future self coming to open the door and welcome you in.

How does your future self greet you? Let your future self invite you into the house. Take a look around the house. What do you see?

What's the feel of the house? What's the feel of this person who's welcoming you into their home?

Your future self invites you for some food and for some drink. They take you to their favourite spot in the house. Again, what do you see? What does it feel like? What's around you? What's the furniture like? What's on the walls?

Your future self is present and ready to listen to you and share with you. Ask your future self what has mattered most over the past 20 years. The nature of the answer may be different They may answer with actual words or you may just get a feeling or a facial expression or some images come to you. You may hear something, you may just feel something but listen carefully. Use whichever of your senses you need to listen. To feel what that answer is. Feel free to ask your future self. What do I need to know to get from where I am to where you are?

Again, listen deeply to the answer. Your future self may answer in words. They may use a facial expression. Or you may just get a feeling in your body that answers the question for you. Ask your future self. What will help me to sing my true song? What will help me to live our life's purpose? Listen deeply to the answers. Feel the quality of the answers? Let those answers surprise you.

While you're here, you can ask any other questions. Big questions, small questions, somewhere in between questions. Ask your future self for guidance. Is there a dilemma you're in at the moment, a tough situation in your life, or anything else that you'd like to hear their perspective about? Again, spend some time really listening, really feel the answers. Now looking deep into their eyes, ask your future self. What's your true name, other than our given name? What name are you called by? Be open to whatever surprising name shows up here. It may make sense to you. And it may not.

Your visit is going to start to come to an end now. You know that you can come back anytime you need to. And that your future self will always be with you. Thank your future self, for their wisdom and the guidance that they've offered you. And then notice as the conversation is coming to an end, that your future self has a parting gift for you. And they're very, very excited to give it to you. Let them bring that gift to you. What's that gift like? Is it wrapped up for you to open another time? Or is it there, available for you to see now. Thank your future self again for their time and for that gift.

Now make your way out of the house. Find your way back to the beam that brought you here. Step onto that beam and let it begin to carry you upward again.

You can watch your future self's home as it gets smaller and smaller beneath you as you move through the clouds all the way back up to that dark blue-black space.

And there, notice the original beam. Step back onto that one and allow it to bring you back down to Earth in the present time. As you travel down start to see the Earth coming back into focus. See the landscape of your part of the world, your country, your region. See your town or your city. From a bird's eye view, follow that beam all the way back down into the room where you began your journey.

Slowly come back into your body. Feel your toes and your fingers. Wiggle them a little bit. Just start to bring some movement back into the rest of your body turning circles with your wrists and your ankles, stretching your arms and your legs. Become aware of the chair or the bed underneath you. When you're ready, take a deep inhale and exhale and very softly open your eyes.

And while you're still in this space, still feeling that connection really strongly to your future self, take your pad and your pens. Jot down the answers to these questions.
- What did you see?

- What was the home like?
- Where was the home?

- Was there anybody else in the home?

- Was your future self living alone?

- What was your future self's presence like?

- What were the questions you asked your future self?

- What was their answer?

- What was your future self's true name?

- And what was their parting gift?

- Did your future self surprise you in any way?

- Did your future self offer a truly different perspective from the one you were previously operating with?

> Spend some time sitting with these questions. And know that you can come back to your future self any time of any day to give you guidance and support in your present-day life.

Now that you have your future self with you, you may well find this is all the download you need - a steer; a compass point; a direction to set for your life. You are now free to give yourself permission to make your decisions according to that knowing.

The reason I'm writing this book and gave it the title I have is that energy and the spiritual arena can be really intimidating. The expression "spiritual awakening" is particularly irritating to me.

Because we're used to the polarity of sleep and wakefulness it implies that one minute, you're asleep and the next you've had every spiritual experience imaginable and are wide awake. Not so.

In my experience, "spiritual awakening" is a slow and steady experience. It's like following a trail and picking up the pieces which after a while begin to form a whole.

I'm 14 years into exploring spirituality consciously and only now is it beginning to really fall into place. Of course, some people have clear awakenings. They may have an ayahuasca experience or take magic mushrooms. I can pretty much guarantee that alcohol will never get you there. Alcohol is one of the most unconscious drugs on the planet. It is like a cosh that will block any possibility of achieving altered states.

I smoked a lot of marijuana when I was young and, thinking back, I was probably quite connected at that time. But when I stopped smoking, my drug of choice became alcohol, and my connection was lost.

Now what I do is meditate. We will look at meditation in much more detail later in the book. For now, I just want to demystify this notion of "spiritual awakening".

Some people do indeed have blinding flashes of sudden knowledge, near-death experiences are an example of that type of change. But for many, myself included, the change is gradual. Words said here, tingles felt there, interesting and remarkable coincidences and synchronicities which keep showing up are great indicators.

The internet seems to me to be an amazing route. The algorithms, knowingly or not, will be supporting whatever change we're looking for. The fact that you're reading this book, especially if you're reading the Kindle version, tells me that, consciously or unconsciously, you have put the energy of inquiry into the Universe. And the Universe, as it does, has lined things up so that you can pursue that line of inquiry. Is that a download? Maybe, especially given that you downloaded this book.

Let's look at what needed to happen between your device and the platform you accessed this book from. In fact, let's back up even further.

I have been reading about, studying and practising personal development since 2004, when my only son died. I needed to put some kind of reason around that. I have accumulated enormous amounts of knowledge and understanding since then, and I have nearly two decades of spiritual exploration and experiences. Some of these experiences were mundane, some earth-shattering, some painful, some wonderful. Ultimately, they led me to the living rooms of two psychics. Both those psychics told me I need to write this book. One of those psychics told me twice.

So, this book and its contents have been swirling around in my field for six months.

Nine days ago, the publisher of this book contacted me, he promised me no big pitch, just clarity - an approach I really like. We spoke. He received [as a download !] the date for publication and the next day I put pen to paper and began to move these teachings through me in the form of this book. With my publisher now holding me to account, not to mention a fairly large chunk of money, I met the deadline for publishing the book and here it is.

That's my side, the delivery side, the give half of the equation. Meanwhile, there is you. You're hearing all this stuff. There's noise in the ether about meditation, guides, higher selves, new paradigms, spiritual awakenings. COVID has taken the planet by storm and your world has been turned upside down or at least sideways. You're looking for answers. You're looking for understanding. The old world doesn't make sense anymore, but you don't know where to turn.

You put a light-hearted search into the largest online bookseller in the world, "spiritual awakening" and up I pop. The title makes you chuckle. You like my face. You like my smile. You like my bio. You look inside. Your interest is piqued. You click to buy - it's only a couple of pounds or dollars – the price of a cup of coffee for Enlightenment – a bargain!

You were ready. I had something waiting for you to receive and the clever tech bits between us connected the dots and your download became available. Synchronicity? Deliberate Creation? Law of Attraction? Who cares? You're reading this book now. Consider this your first download.

Chapter 2
Higher Selves

Your higher self or future self or inner mentor or any number of other names is simply your inner knowing. It's that river of wisdom that runs deep within you. It's your intuition really. There is actually no great mystery. We all have a higher self. It's just semantics and what we choose to call it really doesn't matter.

In fact, if you did the future self visualisation, you just met your higher self. I don't see a difference between my future self and my higher self.

But just to be sure, my higher self has guided me to create another audio file to help you access your higher self. You can access file here https://healingmoney.kartra.com/page/higherself . The reason this book directs you to audio files is that it really is very difficult to write about these things. I practise and teach Kundalini Yoga which we describe as the yoga of experience. I can describe to you what a Kundalini Rising is, but you will never be able to feel it unless you do it. The same is true of these spiritual practices and the best way to access the wisdom of your higher self is to meet them, get to know them and make it a habit to connect with them. I recommend repeating the practice little and often. Culturally we are not encouraged to hone this skill. In fact, culturally, we are at best discouraged and at worst punished for honing this skill.

The fact that you are reading this book tells me you are more than ready to get to know and work with your higher self. I know you are ready, if you haven't before, to get up close and personal with your higher self and to begin to tune in to all that they have to teach you.

So, I invite you now to sit back, relax, close your eyes and listen to the audio.

If you don't have access to the electronic version, you can record yourself reading this transcript, or you can ask a friend or relative to read it to you.

If you, or someone else, is reading the transcript, please do so slowly, calmly and quietly. Leave pauses and create space for the answers to come in. This is a meditation and needs to be done slowly and deliberately. Make sure you have the time to really connect consciously. If you don't have the time right now, I recommend you come back to the mediation at a later time.

Meeting your higher self:
Find a comfortable place to sit. Not too comfortable - we don't want you lying down and falling asleep. Have your back relatively straight, your spine upright. Your head is supported your feet are flat on the ground with both soles connected to the ground.

Ideally, you're barefoot, or you have something like a sheepskin underneath your feet. Try and avoid rubber and plastic because that insulates you from Mother Earth. We want to be channelling energy from the heavens down through the body and into the ground.

Close your eyes and go within. Just become aware of your breathing – the gentle rise and fall of your chest and your belly as you breathe.

Any sounds you hear in your environment, just let them soothe you. Let them be part of this meditation. I'm just going to ask a very simple question. Open yourself up to whatever the response is. I'm just going to ask

"higher self. Are you there? Please show yourself to me in whatever way works".

At this point, you may experience some kind of tingling, you may hear a voice, you may see lights. Or you may just have a deep inner knowing. It doesn't have to be physical. You are not actually connecting with something physical. So, it makes perfect sense that it's not physical, but if it is physical, then that can help too.

Just feel that connection and bring your higher self into your experience. You may want to ask your higher self a question. First of all, ask if it's alright if they're in the mood to talk. It's very unusual for higher selves not to be in the mood to talk with their being.

What would you like to know from your higher self? What can they answer at this moment? Is there anything else that they'd like to tell you?

Is there anything that they'd like you to do? On an ongoing basis. My experience is that, once higher selves have been connected with, they're quite keen that that connection is made often and regularly. They like a sense of surrender and trust. They are your higher self, your future self, your inner mentor, your guidance, your intuition. My experience is that the more deeply we trust, this incredible river of wisdom that is flowing through us, the better we can flow through and navigate our lives.

My higher self is guiding me through this meditation. Some people like to give their future selves or higher selves a name. If that resonates for you, then find out what that name is. Ask your higher self, what would you like to be called? What are you called? How would you like me to refer to you and about you?

Before we say goodbye... And it's not really goodbye because your higher self and your future self and your intuition and your guidance, they're all the same thing. They're always there, always available to you, always there just waiting to give you an answer. So, there's no goodbye.

The more you practise this, the more you will just have that connection instantly without having to do the whole sitting down and getting comfortable. You'll just be able to tune in and say, "Where do I go now?" and some people have the experience ... they might get goosebumps, they might get a little tingle, some people get smells, itchy noses, watering eyes. Sometimes it's not a physical sensation at all. It's just like I said, this inner knowing.

So, trust it. Trust it and surrender to it.

If you didn't have any specific experience today, don't beat up on yourself. Don't beat up on me. Don't beat up on your higher self. It's a practice. It's a practice that we're not familiar with in the Western world, we're not encouraged to learn about this. So, it can take a while.

You know, when you first sat in a car, if you're a driver, you didn't know how to drive as soon as you sat in the driver's seat. You had to learn. And it may be that you have to learn how to connect with your future self because that connection has been cut for many, many, many years, and decades, and possibly even lifetimes.

So go softly with yourself. Come back to the practice whenever you need to. Come back to this audio. Or if you don't like the audio, you can just do it yourself, you know what to do now.
You can just sit quietly and invite your higher self to make themselves known to you. You're tuning into something that's quite different to what goes on in the Zeitgeist, in the Collective Consciousness.

The Collective Consciousness is not tuning into their higher selves. It is an unusual practice and you're trying to find the frequency. It's like you're tuning a radio dial. You're trying to find where your own frequency is, and the more you can tune into your own frequency, the clearer the messages will become.

So now, we're just going to bring this practice to a close.

Taking a deep inhale. And exhale and stretch your body in any way you need to.

When you're ready, opening your eyes and coming back to the physical reality that you're so used to

The higher self is everything that the ego is not. The higher self is also everything that is not programmed by Collective Consciousness.

In yogic science, we learn that the soul comes into the growing foetus 18 weeks into pregnancy. These teachings, as well as those of Western astrology, affirm that the soul is completely deliberate in where and when it incarnates. The teacher who taught me that topic in my yoga teacher training has a very cute story about how his daughter, aged about three, paused while eating her breakfast one morning. She looked up and said to her parents. "I remember before I came. I was looking down and I saw you and I thought, "They look nice. I'll go and join them". I love this story so much. It makes our time here on this planet, so much more meaningful.

The yogic traditions hold that souls come here for lessons, as individuals, and collectively. And many people describe how there is familiarity with other souls that they meet in this life. That familiarity begins with our birth families, and then we meet our childhood friends, some of whom stay for lifetimes. Then later, as we change and develop, we meet our adult friends. Some of these friends stay a long time. Others pass through, as the saying goes, for a reason or a season. As you scan your life, I am sure you will find people who you seemed to just know, on a deep level, as soon as they entered your life.

I recently heard a channelling of Jesus Christ - as you do. I very much trust the medium (Amanda Ellis) who did the channelling. I think she's really got something going on. The message that came through from Jesus was that planet Earth is where our souls come to have a heart experience. There's no other existence, apparently, where our hearts can experience so much pain and also have such an opportunity for opening. So, I would encourage you, while you're on this planet living this life, to keep enjoying the experience that you're having. We all know that sometimes it can be incredibly painful to be a human being. And we all know that at other times it can be absolute bliss. Another famous spiritual teacher (Bruce Lipton), tells his students not to wait for heaven. He tells us that this is heaven and we can all make it be our own version of heaven. It all depends on the choices we make.

I am writing this book to show you that you are in control. This life thing is not just happening outside you. Sadly, you (like most in our society) were shut down from a really early age. But something has brought you to read this book. Some little thing inside you has reminded you that you are not a human being having a spiritual experience. You are a spiritual being having a human experience. I want to help you to understand this spiritual experience more deeply and to make the most of your experience of being incarnated in this human form.

It is actually incredibly exciting. When we get out of our way and stop falling into line with the programming that we are being run by, we suddenly discover that we are the deliberate creator and we can create whatever we choose to.

I'm going to talk a little bit more about this in the next chapter. Although this book is made of chapters (another bit of programming !!), in lots of ways what I am presenting here really is not linear.

In the spiritual realm, there is an enormous amount of crossover. Higher selves, future selves, inner mentors, guides. As we've already seen they are all pretty much the same thing.

We don't need to get bogged down in an overload of detail.

Spirituality, in my opinion, is one of the simplest things. It is your connection to your soul's essence.

Please trust me when I say,

You are a soul. You are an eternal soul, and you are living, oh so briefly, on this planet in this lifetime.

You may have been here for many lifetimes. But for this lifetime, just trust. You can't come to any harm. Your soul will live on when you die, your body is just a container for your beautiful soul.

In Kundalini Yoga, we have many mantras (we will look at this in the meditation chapters). The simplest is Sat Naam and it means quite simply "truth is my identity". Sat Naam evokes that little piece of your spirit that you came with and that you will leave with – it is the truth of you and you can access it through your higher self.

Sat Naam.

Chapter 3
Guides

One of the most disempowering things about our traditional concept of spirituality is that God is somehow outside of us. Institutionalised religions, particularly Christianity, worship a figure, invariably male, who can only be accessed from the outside and by certain people who have received specialist training and teachings.

Because of that, the concept of "guides" bothers me somewhat. It perpetuates this sense of the external.

I believe that we have all the guidance we need inside us. We have it as children. Children innately know what they need to do for their bodies and their health, at any given moment. Their moods precisely track their needs. Their behaviours track their moods. They are honest and expressive and they love themselves very much.

Then we send them off to school. We shut them down. We shut down their impulses. We turn off their intuition. We squeeze them into holes they often really don't want to go through. We make them fit a model.

One of my greatest desires from 2020 into 2021 and all that COVID has brought. (Oh my gosh, I have so many desires from this time!!), but my greatest desire is that we will collectively reassess and redesign our education system so that we can find the space to get back to listening to and hearing our own intuition. We need the space to become super aware. We have to shut out the noise from the outside world. And we need to go within.

Your body is like a radar tracking your needs at any given moment. Imagine yourself walking around the supermarket. Someone bumps your ankle with their trolley and you flinch. That's what's known as a contraction. Your cells literally recoil from the unexpected discomfort.

Now, imagine you're in the street. You're walking along and suddenly in the distance you see someone you love. Your heart opens a little. Your face breaks into a smile. As they get closer, your arms may well open into an embrace. This is an expansion.

You are experiencing micro contractions and expansions every second of every day. These are your guides.

When I began writing this book, I was advised to give every chapter a title in the form of a question. You will notice that I didn't do that. The reason is that questions make us doubt. Intuition comes straight from the right side of the brain. As soon as we stop and ask questions, we are no longer trusting our intuition. We are no longer listening. We are doubting it and it will quickly fade away. This radar is quiet. It's like a whisper. It's okay to question some stuff. In fact, I would argue that it's really very healthy to question a lot of stuff. But not your intuition, not your guidance. Your intuition is your truest compass point. And yet, we have questioned it so much that it has ceased to be valued in our society.

It is that questioning that erodes our capacity to create our own lives. It is that questioning that makes us doubt what we are capable of and we end up giving up on our dreams and living mundane lives – getting drunk on a Friday night, binge-watching box sets and waiting for Monday to roll around so we can get back on the merry-go-round of life. What if I told you it doesn't have to be that way? Oo – a question !! What if I told you that "society" is a farce? What if I told you that you are in choice?

You can decide to bin the whole lot right now and live a different way. You just need to learn to turn inside. When you turn inside, you will know that you have everything you need right here right now. You are breathing. You are alive. That is what you came here to do. The rest is up to you.

I always knew I would write this book. And here it is. But let me tell you, I have had many falterings along the way. The most common question which has blocked me is

"Who does she think she is to write a book?"

Society has taught me, as it has taught everyone on this planet to play small, to shut up and listen – not to my inner guidance but to all the noise in the outside. It started with my family, then school and the church, then the media. I had to make a conscious decision to trust my intuition, to trust what I knew and know is true and to believe that the Universe has my back. It has yours too.

Look around – not just at me but at other people who are standing up and pursuing their dreams. Those dreams come true. They may not manifest instantly. In fact, it would be quite dangerous if everything manifested instantly. We need to take steps to support the Universe in bringing them into physical form. For example, this book did not write itself. I had to step out of my comfort zone and face the prospect of people pulling me down. I had to use time and my resources to write the book. I had a voice inside me telling me to do this and I had voices outside me (the voices that came to me via the psychics) egging me on and championing my abilities.

We all know, on some deep level, what we came down here to do. I believe that we did make soul contracts before our souls came down. When Amanda Ellis channelled Jesus he talked about Judas Iscariot and that the soul that lived in Judas' body was the only one brave enough to take on that awful role of betraying Jesus.

I want to be super clear here. I am not a Christian. I was brought up in the Catholic church until I was 15 although I lapsed way before then. I do not much care for the way the Christian churches have corrupted the teachings that Jesus undoubtedly brought to Earth. I don't like the way churches and other religions have used power and wealth over the people. I do, however, believe that Jesus walked this planet, and I do believe that he was one of the good guys. I believe he walked the land and inspired his followers and, because he was a healer and questioned the authorities - the dark forces, he was put to death most unpleasantly.

I'm not claiming to be a new Jesus. And I don't yet have any embodied knowledge of what I am doing here, or what my soul's contracts are. I do know that I am forever questioning and I seem to have an innate knowledge and understanding about spiritual matters and I know that I am a spiritual teacher. I see my role as demystifying some of the language around "spirituality" and giving people a helping hand on the road to uncovering their own version of spirituality.

In my humble opinion, institutionalised religion has given spirituality a very bad rap. Spirituality is an inside job.

I don't like dogma.

I love hearing people accessing their own truth and expressing their spiritual experiences and connections in a way that resonates for them.
I love authenticity.

I love cherry-picking. There is a whole great big smorgasbord out there. What resonates for one person may not for the next person.

This does not negate it. It just means that we are all 100% unique, energetic beings. We are free. We are free to experience and express God, the Universe, Source, Spirit exactly as it shows up for us.

Ignore the language if it doesn't resonate with you. Ignore the practices that don't resonate with you. Skip over the bits that make you contract and step bravely into the bits that make you expand.

You are a beautiful and unique expression of the Divine.

All the answers are inside you.

Ask the questions. Connect to the answers and trust what you hear.

You are an infinite being. Enjoy your journey here on Earth.

Sat Naam.

Chapter 4
Everyone Can Do This

I love that this is chapter four. In numerology four signifies stability. And stability is what gives these teachings assuredness.

So much in the spiritual world sounds nebulous, etheric and ungrounded.

In Kundalini Yoga, we recognise two realms, the animal realm of the lower chakras, which are represented by the three F's fight, flight and f**k. And the angelic realm of the upper three chakras.

We consider the heart to be the bridge between these two realms.

I'm going to take a little excursion here and explain what the chakras are for those of you who are not familiar.

In the 3D world, i.e. the three-dimensional world we are used to experiencing, we recognise eight chakras.

The **root** is associated with security and stability. It is our places of grounding and is at its strongest when our basic needs - food, water, shelter - are met.

The **sacral** chakra is associated with our creativity. It is situated around the reproductive organs. Of course, the ultimate expression of creativity is a new life.

Next, we have the **navel point** known in Sanskrit as the Nabhi and in Chinese energy work as the Dan Tien. The Nabhi is where our courage comes from. Often when we're moving from creation into manifestation, we need a great deal of courage to push ourselves through from ideas to realisation. We need to push bravely past our growth edge.

Then, we have the heart. Of course, the beautiful heart is a well-known thing and it is being increasingly studied and understood. Do you know that there is more, and I mean significantly more, electromagnetic energy around the heart than there is around the brain? If you measure the energy around a brain, you'll find it extends about one inch beyond the brain. Around the heart, the same amount of electromagnetic can be measured 3 feet away. This is why parents have an instinct when their children are in danger. The connections we have with each other at the heart are some of the strongest and they are not dependent upon being in an intimate relationship. It is perfectly possible to have a strong heart connection with a good friend or even a stranger.

The heart forms a bridge between those lower chakras - the animal realm – and the angelic realm, which begins with the throat.

The **throat** is where our speech comes from. It's where we show up in the world and express our hopes and dreams.

The **third eye** is situated between the eyebrows and is directly connected to the pineal gland which sits in the middle of the brain. The pineal gland contains the same physical structures as the eyes that we can see on our faces. It contains rods and cones like the retina of the eyes we are used to seeing. The pineal gland is also shut down very quickly as we move through childhood and aren't able to make the funny little noises that children love to make. Those shrilling, drilling noises that are made by rapidly vibrating the tip of the tongue on the roof of the mouth stimulate the pineal gland. In children, the pineal gland is plump and healthy. In the average western adult, it is shrivelled and calcified – apart from adults with a strong meditation practice.

At the top of the head, we have the **crown** chakra. The crown chakra, interestingly, is situated at the fontanelle where the four plates of the skull come together. When a baby is born, the fontanelle is still open. The crown chakra is still physically open and babies are still connected to and receiving from Source. As a child gets older, those plates of the skull come closer together and the crown chakra seals over. This sealing over is another part of the shutting down of our connection to our spiritual selves.

Finally, we have the aura. The aura is what extends beyond the body. In fact, it extends around about a metre. If you think about what's been going on in the world with COVID and social distancing it would seem that social distancing is allowing us to really feel and experience our auras. I would suggest that, since COVID struck and we've had to keep our distance from each other, people are becoming much more sensitive to their auric fields.

Chakras are centres of concentrated energy and matter coalesces around frequency so the physical matter has coalesced around these centres of energy.

If you map what we perceive as the physical body onto the chakra system, you will notice organs of extreme importance around each chakra.

At the root, we have the anus and the urethra - the places from which we eliminate waste from the body.

At the sacral, as I mentioned before, we have the reproductive system.

The nabhi is just under the belly button. And of course, the belly button is where we were connected to our mothers, where the placenta and the umbilical cord, joined the mother to the baby.

The heart speaks for itself. If the heart's not beating, you're not living. There are whole libraries written about the heart. As the heart is studied more, it is becoming better understood to be the most important organ in the body, not just physically but emotionally and spiritually too. I encourage my clients and students to breathe into the heart space. As you read this, bring your left hand into the space just in front of your heart with the palm facing towards your body. Feel the energy there. Now take a few deep breaths and direct that breath into your heart space. As I type this, I am breathing into my heart space and connecting with you all.

The old paradigm has very much championed the idea that the brain is the most important organ. As new technologies are being discovered and as we move into the Aquarian Age, the new world, the fifth dimension, we are understanding and appreciating the value of the heart so much more. The heart is the seat of our intuition. It is the heart that we need to settle into, as we make decisions and move forward in our lives. The heart holds the truth and the heart holds love and forgiveness – two of the highest vibrating emotions we experience.

The throat, obviously, contains the voice box, the larynx. There is enormous energetic potential in verbal communication.

The third eye is directly linked to the brain and the eyes on our face. An enormous amount of energy passes through the eyes. When we meditate, we close our eyes. We do that in order that we don't dissipate that energy through the eyes.

And finally, of course, the crown of the head, the fontanelle and the connection to Source.

Yes, everybody can do this. Everybody is intuitive. Everybody has a higher self. Everybody has their inner guidance. But we are so shut down. It has not been the habit of the collective consciousness to explore and to use these incredible abilities. Over the centuries, people have been at best sidelined and at worst punished and even killed for using these skills. They've been tortured, drowned, burned at stakes and hanged for these practices. No wonder in our psyche, the spiritual amongst us has felt a need to hide.

I recently saw a quite incredible documentary. In the film, children were blindfolded. I kid you not, these children were reading word perfectly from a book that, according to our way of viewing things, they could not see. The children could not see with their eyes but other cells were taking over the reading for the eyes.

The really interesting thing was that whenever anybody who was sceptical came anywhere near them, the children's abilities would shut down. It was as if some kind of protective mechanism kicked in to keep the ability under wraps.

The teacher was emphatic about two things:

1. They never ask the children questions. Instead of saying "what do you see on the page", they would say "tell me what you see on the page"
2. The lessons move really fast. There is no space allowed for the left brain to get involved and start questioning what is going on.

It was truly fascinating.

Personally, I have watched people play with energy. I have extracted dark, heavy energy from my clients. I have released my own dark heavy energy and I have learned to train my own energy. I help my clients to train theirs.

I experience energy. I don't see it or smell it or hear it. I sense it. I tend to think of a cat's whiskers when I describe how I experience energy. It's like a tingle – that inner knowing again.

We all have different ways of experiencing this. Remember the contractions and expansions from the last chapter. Imagine you're at a party. You scan the room. You will notice people who you are drawn to and you will notice people who you are repelled by. It's got nothing to do with how they look. It's about their energetic frequency. It's about the subtle messages that are being delivered to you by your guidance system, by your higher self by your intuition.

When you went to school, aged 5, 6, 7, you will have learnt to shut those systems down.

Children innately know when they need to stand; when they need to sit; when they need to lie; or cry; or laugh; when they need to shout; when they need to talk; and occasionally they even know when they need to listen.

But their impulses don't suit our systems. So, they learn to turn their needs off. They learn to fight the impulses in their bodies, the impulses in their energetic field and to conform to what the system wants of them.

We mould our young people to make them fit this crazy world that we have created so that they will blindly stumble into boring jobs in boring organisations, moving unnecessary things around our beautiful planet.

We have disconnected ourselves from the natural rhythms of the planet.

I just Googled "nature definition" and the first result, from Oxford Languages, is:

"The phenomena of the physical world collectively, including plants, animals, the landscape, and other features and products of the earth, as opposed to humans or human creations".

This definition only recently crossed my path. And it has shocked me deeply. We are so disconnected from our natural state that we regard ourselves as in opposition to nature.

When did that happen? Why did that happen? Who has benefited from that happening?

See, I'm asking questions now !!

These are the questions that are important to ask. The innate skills and knowledge that every human being was born with have been systematically crushed out of our experience.

People who have a spiritual practice are described as being woo woo. We're derided for being woo woo. We're marginalised. Over the centuries, and millennia spiritual people have been tortured, and killed for practising these things.

And spirituality was commandeered by institutionalised religions. I was so offended by the Catholic Church's interpretation of spirituality that I spent my teens and early 20s, declaring myself a devout atheist. In my late 20s to early 30s, I began to temper that to agnosticism. When my baby died, I started to wonder if there was maybe something deeper going on and when I felt his soul leave my body when I was around 40, I began to open up. I really began to own my spirituality in my mid-40s, and it was becoming a Kundalini Yoga teacher, which convinced me that we are spiritual beings, having a physical experience and not the other way around.

This is quite a common curve for spiritual awakening. If you've been brought up in a very religious environment, you may find that you'll shun it completely and become an atheist. And then gradually turn yourself into an agnostic. And then finally, declare yourself to be a spiritual being.

Do I remember? - Not yet?

Do I believe I will? - Most definitely.

And am I opening up to remembering? - you betchya.

Chapter 5
Paradigms

Ooh. This chapter is juicy ...

I always wished I'd been 18 rather than a baby in 1969 when the Woodstock Festival took place. Whenever I look at footage of that era, it looks like my era.

As 18 year-olds my friends and I wore long flowing skirts to match our long flowing hair. We were called the hippies, and we were proud. There was something about the hippie era that really resonated with me. Later on, I realised that I was quite grateful not to be alive at that time. A lot of people died. There was a level of misunderstanding and disrespect for what was emerging on the planet and that, I am sure, is why there was such a backlash to it. Maybe it's because there were so many drugs being taken at the time that somehow the energy that was pouring over the planet was not treated with the respect that it deserved.

The hippie era was the start of the switch into the Age of Aquarius, which marks the end of the Piscean Age. The Piscean Age was all about masculine energy. One woman or man for her or himself, sharp elbows, the top of the pile, clearly defined hierarchical structures, us and them, the haves and the have nots. It was an age of limit, of glass ceilings, a sense of lack and not-enoughness. It was full of secrecy and dark energy. Science ran the show with politicians and big business. The Piscean age saw the slave trade and enslavement of the masses.

In the Piscean Age, as soon as a baby was born, it began to be pushed into shapes and spaces that those in charge had chosen for it.

Crikey. As I write this, I'm experiencing pain in my lower back. I can feel the weight of the energy of the Piscean Age. I don't like it one bit. So, I'm going to start writing about the Aquarian Age.

Instantly the energy around me is freeing up. My breath is becoming freer. My writing is flowing more softly. The Aquarian Age is defined by feminine energy. It's the energy of flow and collaboration, community and love, generosity and support. In the Aquarian Age, we look for ways to help each other. In the Aquarian Age, we know that abundance is available to everyone. There is no limit. Resources, when treated with kindness and respect, are unlimited. Have you ever tried to have a vegetable patch for one person? It is not possible. Nature's Bounty is never-ending. She will go on and on giving. There is more than enough for everybody. It's like love. It is infinite.

In the Aquarian Age, we know how to heal ourselves. We make use of our inner technologies. We take care of our bodies, working to prevent disease rather than cure it. We work sympathetically, with our planet. We honour the cycles of the seasons. We allow our land to recover from over-farming. We live in harmony with nature. We take our place back with Mother Nature and we discover what we can learn from her.

In the Aquarian Age, our spirits are free. We are moving gracefully through this lifetime and ensuring a better tomorrow for our children and our children's children. In the Aquarian Age we live for the good of all, we don't cream off, we don't abuse each other. We never enslave one another. We live with respect and love. This is the new paradigm.

A paradigm is defined as a pattern or a model. Paradigms are powerful things. They shape our experiences. I firmly believe that all the trouble we're experiencing on the earth at the moment is the death throes of the old paradigm. It knows its days are numbered, and it is clinging on to power by whatever means it has. Two paradigms cannot exist side by side. We will have to make a collective decision, and we will have to make that decision soon.

At the time of writing this book (April 2021), energy is pouring over our planet again. The far-flung planet of Saturn is transiting Aquarius from 2020-23 and Uranus, which is ruled by etheric and "out there" Aquarius is transiting Taurus between 2019 and 2025. Taurus is all about money, banks and the fixed physical. These opposites will continue to cause energetic upheaval for some time. Pluto will be moving into Aquarius in 2023-24, and then, as above so below, we will be fully lined up for the new paradigm to take over.

We need this. Collectively, we need to breathe again. We need the stranglehold that the Piscean Age has had on us all to be released so that we can relax into this new and loving age.

The old paradigm is not going to give up without a fight though. You've probably noticed. This is what all the polarisation has been about. It began in 2016 with Brexit and has continued since then with the election of President Trump, and finally the big one COVID. This is it guys, this is the wake-up call. That WAS the wake-up call. Whatever you experienced in 2020 because of COVID, that is what has brought you here to read this book.

You KNOW that something else is going on, but you don't know what. It's a bit scary, and you're looking for like-minded and like-hearted souls to move through these troubled waters with.

It's okay. We're here. We've got each other. We just need to breathe and meditate (seriously) and safely navigate this transition time together.

Incidentally, there is something to say here about timelines. I am reliably informed that the timelines have now split and there are two paradigms attempting to occupy the planet currently (April 2021). That is why everything feels so uncomfortable. That is why we have all this polarity and disagreement on the planet.

My advice to you at the moment is to align yourself with the highest vibration people you can find.

We become the sum of the five people we spend most of our time with. If you don't have people in your world who lift you up and support you and support your expanding consciousness, I recommend you find them as soon as possible.

I have a community of like-hearted souls, which you can join by jumping on my mailing list or subscribing to my YouTube channel.

I hold regular connecting spaces. I want you to find YOUR Divine Teacher within YOU. I am happy to lead you and coordinate you, to an extent, but your personal and spiritual development is an inside job. You must take personal responsibility for it.

In brighter news - it's all going to be okay.

Sat Naam.

Chapter 6
Meditation

Meditation changed my life, quite literally.

I had been a stay at home mum for nearly 20 years. I love my children but I was greatly underutilised and greatly undervalued.

I punctuated the boredom and did what I could to make myself feel worthwhile by setting up a little cake baking business. I did okay with that. I do bake a mean cake and I happen to have the best carrot cake recipe in the world in my possession, but I never really felt that this was my calling in life. Baking cakes worked well for bringing up my girls; for receiving them when they got home from school; for listening to their trials and tribulations of the day; for having the house clean and the dinner on the table when my husband came in from work. But for me being the best version of myself - not so much.

Don't get me wrong, I loved, and continue to love, being a mum. My girls are singularly the most precious people in my life. I barely menstruated during my 20s and I was threatened with infertility by a string of doctors. I knew I wanted to be a mum and that threat was quite unbearable to me. Turned out the doctors were way off and I bless my beautiful daughters, and the ease with which they were all conceived, not to mention the fairly straightforward pregnancies and births. By my mid-40s, my inner woman was deeply dissatisfied and I was extremely unhappy. I left my marriage believing that would make the difference but turned out the sadness was inside me not inside my marriage.

In December 2018 I found myself Googling suicide. Fortunately, when you Google suicide, what comes up is help about how to get better not advice on how to take your life. I was offered an online assessment of my mental health. The result came back that I was severely clinically depressed and it was recommended that I go to visit my doctor. So, I made my annual visit to the doctor and, of course, after a five-minute consultation, the doctor gave me - you got it - antidepressants.

Small aside, in 2017-2018 7.3 million people (17% of the adult population) in the UK were prescribed antidepressants (UK government statistics)

During 2015–2018, 13.2% of Americans aged 18 and over reported taking antidepressant medication in the past 30 days. Antidepressant use was higher among women than men in every age group. Use increased with age, in both men and women. Almost one-quarter of women aged 60 and over (24.3%) took antidepressants (Source – Centers for Disease Control, CDC)

The global antidepressants market is expected to grow from $14.3 billion in 2019 to about $28.6 billion in 2020 as mental health issues are expected to surge due to the effects of the Covid-19 pandemic making an impact on the global economy. (Source ResearchAndMarkets.com.)

I had been prescribed these tablets often over the last 10 years. For my Pre-Menstrual Syndrome; for my Season Affected Disease; and for my grief after my stillbirth. This time, I really didn't want to take the tablets. I never liked them and was quite sure there was another way to beat this disease. But I didn't know what else to do and I needed to get out of the headspace I was in – for my girls apart from anything else.

I banished my poor boyfriend, telling him I needed a break for January. A couple of days later I met an old friend in the supermarket. She is a very special friend, the one I went skiing with, one of my greatest teachers. She seems to pop up when I'm in need of a lesson. She grabbed me for a quick cup of tea and said she had been thinking of me. I told her where I was at and she said, "You should go to Osho Leela". I had no idea what she was talking about. Osho what??

I went home and asked another question of Google. I discovered Osho Leela. It's a community in Dorset which lives around Osho's teachings. They host workshops and festivals and they had a "Super Special Weekend" coming up in a couple of weeks' time at the bargain price of £50. I booked it.

Two weeks later, in the depths of January, I drove myself down to the Wiltshire-Dorset borders in my electric car which barely made the journey. I had no idea where I was going and I arrived in the car park, battery on about 5% and so desperate to use the bathroom that I actually relieved myself in a bush behind the car park because I couldn't bear the idea of going in and having that be the first thing I asked.

More comfortable now, I walked through the red door of the house. The door was just shutting on a room called Zorba and someone called to me that the meditation was about to start and did I want to join. I'm an adventurous soul and figured meditation would be fairly low impact so I slipped into the room as they shut the door.

Immediately the lights were turned down low and pulsing house music came up loud. I had missed the intro so all I could do was follow what everybody else was doing and I was rather surprised to find that everybody started shaking. They looked like they were having a good time so I joined in and began my own shaking. The meditation lasted an hour and we went through four phases. I discovered later it was Osho's Kundalini meditation. The stages are shaking, dancing, witnessing and finally lying in stillness listening to Osho's voice, as he talks about heaven on earth, and just how small we are and how big we are all at the same time.

The meditation finished and I followed my fellow meditators to the dinner queue. There was a guy in front of me, a Yorkshire lad. He turned to me and said, "ee there's 'owt like a good shake now is there?" That made me laugh. We ate dinner and the conversations were rich and a little scary in places. I wasn't exactly sure where I had rolled up but I was open to whatever happened.

The reason the weekend was so reasonably priced was that we were required to do some maintenance jobs around the house and the grounds. I needed to be outside as I know that daylight is great for relieving depression. So, I got myself on a team with a few guys - one of them I'm still very good friends with [hi Dale].

We were tasked with cleaning, weatherproofing and erecting a salvaged shed. It is the first thing I see whenever I go back to Osho Leela and it brings back very happy memories. As we worked, we got to know each other, and I came face to face with the funk I was in. I realised that the funk wasn't about a chemical instability in my brain. It was that something was missing from my life. I became aware that some part of me was completely unrealised.

As part of the package and in return for our hard work, we were guided through two other meditations over the weekend. We did a Dynamic Meditation on the Saturday and on the Sunday, I had my first experience of the AUM. AUM stands for Awareness and Understanding Meditation. During the two-hour meditation, we were guided, in a safe and supportive environment, through 14 aspects of the human experience: hatred, forgiveness, love, stamina, life energy, chaos, dance, sadness, laughter, sensuality, chanting, silence, respect and sharing.

These incredibly powerful meditations gave my body permission to release the pent up emotions that it had been holding on to because of societal pressure for decades. I discovered the incredible power of connecting with rather than suppressing my emotions.

The AUM is the pillar of the community at Osho Leela. In fact, the member of the community who facilitated the meditation for us suggested that if every human on the planet had the opportunity to do an AUM at least once a month and ideally once a week, there would be no more war and no more conflict. During the AUM there is no place to hide and the shared experience demonstrates that we all have these emotions. Everyone in the room was able to exhibit those 14 facets of the human experience. The AUM is a great leveller.

The other thing that I discovered at Osho Leela was the power of connecting with other like-hearted souls. Osho Leela is famous for hugging. Not any old hugging but deeply connected, knowing hugging.

Before you start a hug at Osho Leela, you look the other person in the eye. Your energies meet and you feel each other. And then you move into an embrace which is held in a very specific way so that your hearts meet. You can feel the beat of each other. It's tender. It's deep. And it's profoundly different to the cursory hug one might give across the table at a pub for example. It's the real meeting of the beings that those two people are. It's an energetic exchange. It's a meeting of souls.

No words are shared. The energy moves through the eyes and the heart. Most people have experienced this kind of energy exchange with a lover but it's really different when you do it with a stranger. It's not a sexual thing.

It's a soul thing. It really is quite beautiful, and, in my humble opinion, we don't have enough of it.

We're so busy rushing around from errand to errand from consumption to consumption. We simply don't give ourselves the gift of really experiencing each other. I'm quite sure that in lives beyond this earthly one our souls interact like that all the time and that is why it can feel so lonely down here on Earth.

After the transformative weekend at Osho Leela, I stopped taking those tablets and have not taken them since. I never liked them. I always knew I could create what I needed from the inside and I was so happy in this deeply connected place. It wasn't a chemical imbalance in my brain. It was a lack of true connection in my life. I, like so many middle-aged women and men, was simply keeping myself afloat. But my inner needs were not being met by my everyday life. When we slow down, we get to feel each other and ourselves more deeply.

In early February, I went back to Osho Leela, and I learnt a type of tantric breathing. I learnt the masculine and the feminine versions. I learned how to wake myself and my energies up from the inside using breath, sound and the body. It was so beautiful that I decided to take the method home with me and to practise it every day. I just wanted to keep that energy alive and awake inside me.

Sadly, the wonderful meditations and connections I discovered at Osho Leela are hard to come by in our fast-paced world. Our society doesn't lend itself to the type of experiences I had just had so I set about finding it where I could. I soon discovered that Kundalini Yoga was a pretty good substitute for what I had been experiencing at Ohso Leela. It is another fabulous way to get in touch with the energetic body.

Two weeks later, a friend of mine told me about an awesome teacher, Gloria Latham, who was coming to the UK from Canada to deliver a workshop over the last weekend of February. Again, it worked with my dates and I was hungry for any experience which would top up my energetic body. I had the money in my account. [Funny, I always seem to have money for personal development!] so I booked.

At this stage, I really had no idea what to expect from a Kundalini Yoga workshop. I'd done the three classes previously but that was all the Kundalini I had experienced. So, I got myself up to Triyoga in Camden and a tiny tanned Canadian-Greek woman strolled into the studio - no white clothes, no turban, she didn't even tie up her hair which is considered quite sacrilegious by some in the Kundalini world. I liked her!

The entire weekend revolved around one mantra. SA TA NA MA.

Of course, I received all the lessons in exactly the right order. I had been doing the breathing practice every day for the last two weeks and the result of that was to keep the previous workshop alive in me.

I was beginning to figure it out. My happiness was inside me not outside. I was in choice about whether or not to do the breathing. I could have just gone back to my old habits of unconsciously stumbling through my days and wondering why I felt so miserable. I made a different choice. I CHOSE not to. I CHOSE a conscious practice and I CHOSE to keep expanding, finding whatever experiences I could, which would maintain this expansion.

SA TA NA MA or Kirtan Kriya is THE meditation of change in Kundalini yoga. The sounds are the primal sounds, and they represent. Birth - SA, life - TA, death - NA, rebirth -MA.

Gloria invited us if we were looking to change something in our lives, to bring to mind someone who drove us nuts. Maybe a neighbour, a relative, a colleague or partner. It really didn't matter. What mattered was to identify what quality in that person drove us nuts. She explained that it was like looking in a mirror, whatever quality that person is expressing is a quality we hold in ourselves which we don't like, and are ready to release.

She then invited us to think of someone we admire, and what quality that person expressed that we admire.

We all know that nature abhors a vacuum so, in releasing the quality that drives us nuts we make space to bring in the quality we admire. The meditation, coupled with several alarms a day reminding me of what I wanted to change marked the start of me consciously creating the life I wanted.

FYI, the person who irritated me at the time (who shall remain nameless) exhibited the quality of laziness. And the person/people I admired were my second daughter and my then-boyfriend because they are both extremely hard workers.

I finally understood what was happening in my life. I knew I was capable of much more than I was achieving at that time, but I was being lazy. I was being lazy and doing nothing, so I wasn't getting results. This led me to feel bad about myself and knowing I was capable of so much more. But I kept being lazy and I kept not achieving anything and I kept feeling bad about myself, and on and on. Can you feel the energy of that downward spiral?

Of course, I was depressed. I was doing what so many in the western world do. I was looking for some kind of magic bullet from outside my life, that would turn things around. And it never came. Of course, it never came because it isn't outside. I was looking in the wrong place.

What I discovered was the power I had (and continue to have) to change my life from the inside. What I discovered is that happiness is an inside job.

We were tasked with going off and practising this meditation, every single day for 40 days. Gloria was very clear about the 40 days, which had to be CONSECUTIVE.

Later, when I did my own Kundalini Yoga teacher training, I discovered why it has to be consecutive. If you give up 10, 15, 20, 30, 35 days in, you reinforce your inability to show up for yourself regularly. Gloria told us a story of a man who got to day 38 over and over again. He was on his third marriage. This man could not (or would not) consistently show up for himself.

Self-love starts with showing up for yourself - over and over again. I'm not talking about doing it for hours on end - just 10-15 minutes a day. That consistency gives a message to the people around you, and most importantly, it gives a message to you, that you matter, that you matter enough to receive the gift of 10 to 15 minutes a day.

At that stage in my life, I was so bored with myself. I was bored with knowing that there was more to me, and I was bored of being unable to find that more of me. I remember thinking to myself, "40 days, it's not that long, it's just over a month, I can do that".

I didn't have much else going on in my life, see above. I had already discovered how powerful it was to do the breathing every day and after the workshop, I was already three days in. 40 days would bring me to the third of April. It seemed like quite a good way to get through March so I continued.

I did my 40 days. I had my alarms going off four times a day with the label "release laziness and bring in hard work".

I did it. I did 40 days. After 40 days I was ready for a new meditation. So, I did a different meditation now for another 40 days. I began to seek out Kundalini Yoga wherever I could find it. I liked it, I loved it.

One day, I went to a class in Soho and met an excitable lady, also called Emma. She was hosting a retreat over the summer solstice weekend in Yorkshire. She thrust the flyer into my hand. I liked this Emma and the retreat looked amazing. I decided to go and took my oldest daughter.

By the time I got to the retreat in Yorkshire, I'd been meditating for 119 days.

> It takes 40 days to break a habit
> It takes 90 days to make a new habit
> It takes 120 days to master a habit
> It takes 1000 to become a habit

On that retreat, I mastered the habit of meditating, and I set my intention to become a Kundalini Yoga teacher.

I began my training in September of that year and passed my 1,000th consecutive day of meditation in November 2020.

I am now a Kundalini Yoga teacher, a spiritual teacher, a healing business coach and mentor, an Akashic Records reader and a meditation !!

What could you be?

Chapter 7
How To Meditate

I am pleased to say that there are more resources on the internet about meditation than you can shake a stick at. This is great news. This tells me that there is a huge appetite for spirituality and the great awakening going on across the planet. Of course, this is completely obvious. If you peep just a little bit under the surface, you can find videos about crystals and the Law of Attraction on Tik Tok, being made by young people. YouTube is littered with meditation, spirit channellings, astrology and Russell Brand! Plus, COVID and all that the pandemic has led to has been a fantastic opener across the globe. It has been an opening for us to pause, reset, reassess, and change direction.

Many, many people are making the choice to change direction. Many, many people are taking advantage of this hiatus to decide where they want to be, what they want to be doing, how they want to be spending their time and their money. Many, many people are taking advantage of this slowing down to appraise their lives, and the choices they have made, the choices they continue to make and the choices they will make.

In pregnancy, when a mother first starts to feel her baby kicking, it's called the quickening. When my baby died in my uterus, I stopped feeling his kicks. I called that the slowening. I'm sure you can imagine that those were pretty desperate days. He stopped moving on Thursday, the first of July and was cut from my belly on Sunday, the fourth of July. That might sound a little ruthless. But those were actually some of the most important hours I spent with him. I lay in a hospital bed. My older daughters were being taken care of by my sister and my mum for which I am eternally grateful. And my then-husband and I spent time together with our little boy, in "room 2". Room 2 was a little sanctuary. It was in a quiet corner of the maternity ward and the time we spent there was a gift. We were able to stop the world for those few days and honour our baby's short life. I now understand that those days were a kind of meditation. They were still. They were intimate. They were quiet and they were profoundly important to us all.

It doesn't really matter how you meditate. You may decide to use a Kundalini Yoga meditation, with or without a mantra. You may decide to just sit quietly and tune in to the quiet all around you and within you and notice what you can hear or sense.

I do encourage you, if you really want and are ready to get in touch with your spirituality, to develop a meditation practice. It is THE quickest route out of the animal realm and into the etheric realms.

Here's a YouTube link to me teaching Kirtan Kriya https://www.youtube.com/watch?v=OFgvKbCs4jc, the meditation that I took home for 40 days back in February 2018. In this video, I'm specifically using the meditation around money. And there's a good reason for this, which we'll find out more about in chapter 11.

Whatever meditation you do choose to do, I encourage you to take it on for 40 consecutive days. I also encourage you to do the same one for 40 days. You will greatly enhance your practice by keeping a journal as you go through the 40 days. It is a challenge in our ever-changing world to really settle into one meditation for 40 days. Of course, the monkey mind will tell you things like "This is boring". "I know this already". "We've already done this". And it might ask you "What's the point of this?"

What some might describe as boring is actually where some of the deepest transformations are able to happen. I'm involved with a project called Silence With, here's the link. https://www.silencewith.com/ In this experience, the focus of a virtual theatre of silence takes centre stage in silence or song or chatter, or whatever comes up for them for 40 minutes. One night our Zoom call was bombed. The bombers were underwhelmed by what we were up to. "What's the point of this?" "Oh my god, this is so boring." were two of the more polite contributions they hurled aggressively into our space of peace and quiet. The bombers completely missed the point. The point IS to be bored. The point is to find out what is beneath the boredom, what is within the boredom, what is within the silence.

I gather that Clubhouse, the trendiest app on the block, is seeing a rash of silent rooms. We need the silence. We need stillness. We need to sit in meditation to drop down the levels of consciousness which ironically, take us up the levels of consciousness. We have been blocking our consciousness with all the noise and all the activity and production and consumption of the last several centuries. We have the opportunity now, collectively, to experience the stillness. I have not spoken to one person, young and old alike, who did not find some pleasure and comfort in the quiet of the lockdowns we have been experiencing over the last year. I know people have also become bored and frustrated by them, but I believe this is more about the imposition than the actual stillness.

I invite you to make your own choice to find stillness in your head, your heart, your body and your soul. I grew up with Desiderata on my wall. It opens "Go placidly amid the noise and the haste and remember what peace there may be in silence".

The most dangerous words in any aspect of personal and/or spiritual development are "I know that".

In order to grow and expand your consciousness, you must always be prepared to look for more. Open yourself to the answers of the Universe. The best way to do that is with silence and stillness.

In Kundalini Yoga, we start our classes by tuning in with the Adi Mantra:

>Ong Namo Guru Dev Namo.

The words mean:

>I bow to the creative wisdom
>I bow to the Divine teacher within

You cannot possibly hear the voice of the Divine teacher within unless you make your internal landscape quiet, even just for 10 or 15 minutes a day. It's the silence and the stillness that lets the quiet voices of your higher self, your guides and your intuition be heard.

As I said before, it really doesn't matter which meditation you choose. As you begin your practice, you may find that chanting mantra is a useful way to quiet the monkey mind. The monkey mind can't do both. It can't chant and fret about all your worries and your to-do list at the same time. That is why chanting is such a useful way to quiet the monkey mind.

Chanting mantras has another huge benefit. Chanting causes the tongue to strike the upper palate. There are 84 meridian points on the roof of the mouth, and when the tongue strikes these meridian points, they stimulate glands in the brain, which then secrete the various hormones in adjusted quantities and literally change the chemical composition of the brain. Some of the key glands which are affected are the pituitary and hypothalamus glands. These glands are responsible for hormonal activity and for regulating other systems in the body. The key ones are the parasympathetic nervous system, which calms you down, and the digestive system. Meditation affects not just your brain, but your entire body.

Meditation also stimulates one of my favourite glands - the pineal gland which I spoke about earlier in the book. Remember? It is situated bang in the centre of the brain. It contains the same cells (rods and cones) as the eyes we see on the front of the face. It's a lovely plump organ in children and people with a strong meditation practice. However, in most adults, it is shrivelled and calcified. Some theories suggest that fluoride is responsible for that calcification. I have not researched the fluoride question deeply (though others have), but I do know that some of the noises that children make which involve striking their upper palate with their tongues come naturally to the children and are discouraged by parents and teachers.

As you meditate you open yourself up to receiving energy from the Universe. You can decide exactly where you want that energy to come in. If you choose to bring it in through your crown chakra, it will come down into the brain and into the pineal gland. When it hits the pineal gland, you can change its direction by focusing at the back of the third eye (the point between the eyebrows) and project the energy out towards the horizon and the future. In this way, you can harness and direct the energies of the Universe to project the future you're going to co-create with the Universe. This is the beginning of manifestation – seeing your vision and inviting the Universe to support you in creating it.

We are deliberate creators and we are here to have the most expansive experience possible here on earth. The problem is no one has taught us how.

Chapter 8
Can Anybody Do This?

This is the only chapter, whose title is a question. And really, the question should be "why doesn't everybody do this?".
The answer really is very simple. We weren't taught to do this.

Imagine a little baby. It has just been born. Its connection to the ethers is strong. It is still more of a soul than it is a human and it spends hours and hours sleeping, reconnecting to the higher frequencies and vibrations of the soul dimensions.

When there is discomfort in this little soul's physical life it cries. If it can't sleep because of all the noise in its environment, it will become fractious. If its tummy hurts from hunger or trapped wind it will cry. This little being is shocked to be trapped in this low vibration physical body, and it hasn't yet mastered speech, so it cries. It soon becomes apparent, that no one in this baby's world wants it to cry. It gets better and better feedback from what's available in the physical world when it laughs and chuckles. And when it begins to master this strange body that it is encased in, the soul figures out rolling, and crawling and walking and exploring. But so much of the exploration is prevented and curtailed by the adults, protecting the little soul. So, the soul learns to stop its exploring – both the physical and the spiritual.

The baby is gradually made to be busier and busier. It starts with toddler groups then nursery school. It is subjected to an endless stream of stimulation. Then the instructions begin - the programming.

> Sit here.
> Move that.
> Sort these.
> Count those.
> Read this.
> Sit down.
> Stop dreaming.

Come into this world, where we only deal with the lower frequencies and vibrations.

Let's revisit the chakras a bit here. As you read (or listen) I'd like you to bring your attention down to your root chakra. If you're not sure, it sits at the very base of your torso at the perineum. The perineum is a thick muscle situated between the anus and the opening of the vagina in women, and the anus and the scrotal sac in men. Can you feel how dense the energy is there? This is where babies' energy is pulled down to. The root chakra is associated with belonging in the physical realm. When we are in the root chakra, we are looking for safety and security. A human baby needs all the security it can get. Its focus is on staying safe. It cannot survive without its adults and it needs to do what the grown-ups around it expect of it.

The baby is like an unprogrammed computer. As a newborn, it has the most incredible potential to become anything. Imagine the complexity of learning a language. We all know that babies simply soak up and reproduce the language that they experience. If you were to take any baby to a different environment, it would simply learn the new language.

Generation after generation we've concentrated on one thing. We've concentrated on the conscious part of our selves. We've operated and taught from the left brain, analytical standpoint, and this is such a huge mistake. The conscious brain is pretty awesome. It can process 40 bits of information per second. But the subconscious brain leaves the conscious brain standing. The subconscious is processing 20 million bits of information per second.

Do you see the problem here? We're limiting ourselves to one mode of working. We in the West are completely ignoring all the potential of the subconscious brain. Worse, we're not just ignoring it, very often, we're denying it and suppressing it. Think of a young child who's chatting away to their imaginary friends. Can you hear their parents, siblings, teachers, grandparents, and other community members, shutting those conversations down? I had an imaginary friend when I was at primary school. It was a white horse called Lightning. She would wait for me outside school and we would canter home together. Lightning was fiercely loyal but I remember my brothers sniggering behind their hands at me. They may even still be doing so as they read this four decades later. [Hello boys!!].

I was lucky. I was never punished for having my otherworldly stuff going on. Just mocked, to a greater or lesser extent. By the time I went to secondary school, I had given up on my parallel universe. It was safer to fit in. And that is what has happened throughout the centuries - to much greater minds and thinkers than me.

Between 1545 and 1563, The Council of Trent was formed. A group was beginning to form at the time of Natural Philosophers. These were early scientists. The heads of the religions decided that these Natural Philosophers would be separate from religion. It was decreed that religion would be in charge of the soul, the spirit and consciousness, while the natural philosophers would concern themselves with the physical world and materiality.

A very challenging period then unfolded which was overseen by the Inquisition. During this time Natural Philosophers (scientists) were severely punished if they dared to suggest a cross over between the physical and spiritual worlds. Galileo, for example, was held and tried under house arrest and Giardino Bruno, who suggested that the stars were far-flung suns and that there might be other life forms in the Universe, was burnt at the stake for his (heretical) ideas.

With the Inquisition busily torturing and killing any scientists who strayed into the more etheric territories of spirituality, up until 1826, most scientists simply spent their time avoiding this contentious area. They put up, and they shut up and the two paths of science and spirituality grew progressively further and further apart.

This became more insidious as the church grew more powerful. Women in particular (and some men) who had *"other"* sight and knowledge - the healers, the witches, those who were in tune with nature's rhythms and cycles, those who knew how to harvest nature for healing purposes - these women were weeded out. They were ducked, they were burned at the stake, they were hung drawn and quartered. They were imprisoned and tortured. Their heads were exhibited on stakes at city gates. There was more putting up and more shutting up. Witches hid their gifts and abilities and took them underground. They had to hide, or they risked their lives.

The quickest ways to shut down intuition are:

1. **Engage the rational mind, the left brain, with questions.** The rational mind relies on scanning past and future events whereas the subconscious mind only looks at the present moment. The subconscious mind is 500,000 times faster than the rational mind. It makes decisions in the instant. It doesn't analyse. But we have been trained to dredge through the outcomes of the past and to try to predict the future from past outcomes. What a waste of time.
2. **Strong emotions** - especially fear and over excitement. The Inquisition was definitely on to something. When they kept those wise women and men living in fear, the witches quickly lost the connections to their subconscious and intuition. Hmm, interesting. One might argue that that is going on at the moment too. There's an awful lot of fear around on the planet at the moment. Fear also suppresses the immune system which makes people even more susceptible to whatever viruses and bacteria might (or might not) be around.

3. **Doubt.** With questions and fear combined it doesn't take much to pull apart those instincts. As soon as we are called upon to justify our instincts and our intuition, their power is lost.

4. **Busyness.** Intuition is quiet. It needs space around it, it needs stillness and quiet. Remember, our baby who would sit for hours to reconnect to the soul dimensions. From age 3 to 7 years that child is so busy with school, after school clubs, technology, TV etc that it never gets the chance to just be, and tune in. I would love to see meditation being practised in schools – from the earliest age possible. Steve Jobs, a pretty successful and intuitive individual, used to remove his shoes and go walking around the grounds of Apple headquarters when he needed inspiration. Being barefoot meant he had to slow down. And in that slowed down space, many of his best insights and ideas came in. Other geniuses who were at their most creative after periods of stillness are Pablo Picasso and Leonardo Da Vinci who would both stare at blank canvases for hours before going into a frenzy of activity and creating their masterpieces. Nicolas Teslar "saw" the electric motor so clearly

that he instructed his workers to build it in its entirety – no prototype – he just knew that it was going to work.

5. Ego. Oh, hello ego. We haven't talked about you yet, have we? The ego is probably the most damaging and limiting aspect of the average human life today. The ego is the part of us that is always trying to prove something to itself and the next person. The ego causes a lot of pain. It keeps us small, it keeps us in fear, it keeps us limited. Let go of your ego and you will feel freedom like you have not known in this lifetime.

You are meant to be great. You are meant to be the greatest expression of yourself here on this planet.

Come out of the old paradigm and see what is going on in the new. It's really very exciting.

Chapter 9
Shifting Consciousness

I'm writing this book because I want to help millions of people understand and tap into their unlimited potential.

As a Kundalini Yoga teacher, I know that I am supposed to lead from my heart. I am here to support others as they step across the bridge from the animal realm of the lower chakras, to the angelic realm of the upper chakras. And the heart is that bridge. When I met my future self, back in 2016, the gift she gave me was our heart, wrapped in a red silk purse and tied with a golden cord. The heart was beating softly like a tiny bird. Five years later, I finally understand her message. It is clear that I am supposed to lead from the heart. I have been hearing a lot about Jesus recently. Remember his message that this life, on Earth, is all about learning from the heart. On planet Earth, we can have our hearts more hurt than in any other existence and we can open our hearts more here than in any other existence.

Currently, about 10% of the world's population are open to what I and others are saying. Three years ago, that percentage was only 5%. Energy is streaming onto our planet at an incredible rate at the moment. This energy is offering a massive consciousness upgrade.

If I had tried to write this book five years ago, I would have been laughed out of the publisher's office. Five years later, my publisher came to me and when I told him about my book, he said "The world needs this". We're living at such a wild time in human evolution. People are waking up all over the planet. They are questioning the old ways and genuinely entertaining the possibility of doing things differently.

I'm going to carry on our journey of the chakras at this point.

Between birth and seven years, it's all about the root. This is also where, to date, we have put down the lion's share of the programming of our young people.

Between ages 7 to 14, we come into the sacral chakra. The sacral chakra is about creativity and is governed by water. This is the stage of flow and freedom. In recent times, it has been the stage that our poor young people have been put under the greatest pressure to conform. By the time they get into the sacral chakra, their hard drive is pretty much installed. They are used to doing what they're told, and they are in a reactive state. That incredible potential for creativity is by-passed. We shut down our children and force them into the moulds we have created.

From 14 to 21, we come into the navel - the point of courage. This is where more programming happens, where expectations are truly limited and limiting beliefs are firmed up. Parents do this not to be mean. They are well-intentioned. They really think they are doing the right thing. They believe they are protecting their children from hurt and disappointment. They are only recycling the programming they grew up with. Hey, what if hurt and disappointment are exactly the lessons we need to make us grow to be our biggest and best selves? What if we encouraged our young people to take a risk and to be different and creative and imaginative? This is the time we start testing our children. We start labelling them, and yes, we are busy creating here - we're creating small lives, a lack of ambition, comfort and boredom. We allow our young people to drink alcohol and stupefy themselves with hours of swiping on mindless apps. Only a very few young people and their parents are brave enough to question the collective programming and do things differently. Madonna was one of those. Look what happened to her.

This is exactly the time, we SHOULD (and I use that word advisedly) be allowing our young people the freedom to be exactly what they came here to be, not squeezing them through holes into the shapes of the old paradigm.

Does anyone remember Pink Floyd's The Wall? I grew up on that film and album. There is one particular image in the film where masked identikit school children are marching blindly into a machine. They come out the other end minced up as sausage meat. Just imagine if we allowed our children to express themselves, to use the courage and strength of their navel point to create what they came to create. Imagine if we made space for them to listen to their intuition. All that physical power of youth, combined with creativity. The world would be so rich if we let our young people be open to listen to their guidance and to have fun. Then they could come graciously into their hearts.

From 21 to 28, this is where the heart takes over. With different programming, these young people would be able to extend the extraordinary energy of the heart into the world. They would be able to live in love, not fear. They would hear the pulse of the planet. And they would flow. I have a vision. I see our young adults responding in the moment and noticing what the universe is sending their way.

There are six steps to spiritual wisdom:

1. Be receptive. Let it come to you

2. Slow down.

3. Know your inner critic, so that you can distinguish it from your intuition

4. Tune into your body and identify where your intuition speaks to you from. For some, it's the heart. Some the gut. It's not from the head! Track this, so you get used to trusting.

5. Ask for guidance and LISTEN.

6. Take action and become a leader

There are people across the planet, who are using these principles and shunning the old paradigm. They are having incredible results. People you will almost certainly know include:

- Vishen Likhiani (founder and CEO of Mindvalley)
- Oprah Winfrey
- Richard Branson
- Steve Jobs

These people act from a few simple principles which I encourage you to live from too.

Flow. Act in the moment. Respond to what comes in. Notice what you are noticing, and notice the results. Keep doing more of what gets the results.

Observe – who do you bump into? What obstacles do you encounter?

Welcome failure. Failure provides you with challenges and challenges offer you lessons and lessons lead to growth.

Question the old paradigm.

Do more than think positive - **BE POSITIVE**

Live from love. Love eliminates fear.

Live in harmony with the planet and enjoy its beauty.

Know that you control your life and take that control.

Be a creator, not a reactor.

What a different feel there is to living from the heart, from love, rather than fear. If you live from a place of gratitude and acceptance of what is, you can release fear.

Fear is a highly charged emotion, and because it has a very low vibrational frequency and matter coalesces around frequency, being in fear is like saying a prayer for everything you don't want. Energy flows where focus goes, so the more you concentrate on what you don't want the more of it you will get.

Please, just for a moment, imagine a world where we're all free to focus on what we love. A world where we create and exchange from love. Most babies are created in love. And that's such a gift. Imagine if you will, a new world.

Sat Naam

Chapter 10
Abundance and Manifestation

You have abundance right here, right now. You're reading this book or listening to this book, either on some kind of electronic device or in paperback. To get hold of this book, you will have opened, either a different or the same device. You will have used the incredible technology of the internet, almost certainly wirelessly. You are probably in a nice warm home with clean running water, electricity, gas. It's a pretty safe bet that you have lots of mod cons in your life - a kettle, a toaster, an oven, a TV, a car, etc, etc. I imagine your home is safe, warm and well furnished. You get what I'm driving at right?

We're living in a time of incredible abundance and prosperity. And yet so many people feel so poor. The quickest route to increasing your abundance is to be grateful for the abundance you already have. Remember. Energy flows where focus goes. This is the most basic and fundamental principle for expanding your physical experience.

When the Pilgrim Fathers arrived in the Americas, they started banging on at the Native Americans about heaven. And the Native Americans were shocked. They looked at the Pilgrim Fathers bemused and said, "hang on, we thought we already were in heaven".

Heaven or Hell on Earth, you choose. Really, it's as simple as that and every day offers a little bit of heaven. You can actively choose to see it and you can actively choose to seek it out, find it and give thanks for it. Your seeking won't lead you to fire and brimstone. What you will experience is a warm fuzzy feeling of comfort and joy, and you will experience more abundance because you're turning your attention to it. You will notice it more. You will see it in the corners of your life where you never thought to look.

You'll see it in your interactions with your partner, your family, your friends, your colleagues, and most importantly, you will feel your own abundance. You will find that place in your heart where you can notice the abundance you have lived with to date. You will experience abundance in the moment and you will be aware of the abundance that you are now opening yourself up to receive.

Have you ever seen a rosebush refuse to grow more flowers? Have you ever tried to have a vegetable patch for one person? It's impossible. Nature gives and gives and, contrary to popular belief, we humans are part of nature. We have taken our eye off the ball with our consumption and our materialism. A lot of what we produce and consume has indeed been produced without affording our dear Mother Earth the respect she deserves. In spite of that, she's still supporting us.

Abundance doesn't have to be private jets and yachts and five-star hotels. Of course, it can be, but it is really important that we get things in perspective, and share our planet sympathetically, with other life forms.

And you know what? When we slow down and enjoy the precious moments and the abundance we already have, that becomes so much easier to do. When we live in gratitude and acceptance of the moment we are living in we no longer feel the need to fill a vacuum in our hearts with things. When the heart is full of gratitude and love, there's peace, which no amount of material possession can substitute. Love is the answer.

I'm going to talk a little bit about manifestation here.

I used to think I had very little in life. And guess what, I had very little in life because that's where I was turning my attention. When I look back on my life, I realise that I have manifested the most incredible things.

We can manifest misery (and lots of us do) if that's where we put our focus. I manifested a lot of misery. I also manifested my ex-husband, with whom I had a long and happy marriage until the happiness ran out.

When I first started to get consciously into manifestation, I wrote something called a Dream Day Journal every day. For several weeks I wrote about a room that I wanted to wake up in. The room had a huge bed with crisp white sheets and I wrote about myself padding across the sumptuous carpet to a bathroom with a roll-top bath. For my dad's 80th birthday, he rented a house in the Lake District which was a converted hotel. The bedroom I stayed in was the room I had been manifesting and more. It was enormous. There was a huge bed with crisp white sheets. The room was even better than the one I had been writing about. It had sofas and an en-suite bathroom with yep, you got it, a roll-top bath. It's true that I didn't own that room, but I *experienced* that room and I took the trouble to notice that I was experiencing it.

Right now, as I write this, I am in Dorset in the UK. I'm sitting in the sunshine transcribing the pages of this book that I wrote sitting on a beach yesterday.

I wrote the following on the 19th of January 2021. It was my script for the next 90 days.

[Yesterday was the 19th of April 2021 - Monday morning 90 days later…]

"I arrived here yesterday having visited the Maumbury rings in the afternoon. I'm at Waterfield bed and breakfast. [I didn't actually visit the rings on Sunday, but I did go to see them on Monday.]

I can see the expansive countryside of Dorset, which is fresh and green in the warmth of spring. I see the stream meandering by, fish in the water, birds flying high, flowers coming into bloom. [Now I don't know about the fish in the stream, but there are fish on a piece of art in the room that I'm in]. I can feel the warm morning sun on my skin, a gentle breeze brushing through my hair and my lover gently stroking my shoulder as he slips past me [well my lover hasn't quite materialised, but I'm making do with the sun because he is my first love !!]

I can hear the stream gently flowing past, the birds calling in the sky. And my lover's voice whispering softly into my ear. [My lover is me. I've become my own lover in the last three months].

I can taste the delicious breakfast that has just been served to me, poached eggs on mashed avocado and fresh fruit salad. [I got the poached eggs which were delicious !! I didn't get avocado, but I did have delicious toast. And I had the most amazing fresh fruit salad, exactly as I wrote, and I had a warm croissant and tasty muesli].

I can smell the freshly brewed coffee that is being served with breakfast. [I've largely stopped drinking coffee since January so I didn't smell that in the end].

I'm so grateful for everything that has happened, for all the support I've been receiving, and I can't wait to find out what is next in the coming 90 days.

That is a perfect example of deliberate creation. I set the intention back in January that I would be here. And I worked and worked to make it happen. I created an online summit. I've created an online course, written this book and launched a YouTube channel. I've done four massive things.

I set my compass and have taken the actions which indicate to the Universe that I'm serious and then I have surrendered control.

There is a popular misconception about manifestation.

People think that you just say a little prayer for something and up it pops. Firstly, you have to really feel what it is you want to manifest. You have to embody it so that you experience it with all five of your senses so that you can feel the excitement of having those things in your life. Secondly, and this is the bit people tend to miss, you have to take action.

You see, if the Universe manifested every single thing that we put out a call for, we'd be tripping over all sorts of debris that we don't really want. We would be tripping over ex-lovers. We would be tripping over boxes of paraphernalia that in an idle moment we kind of fancy. We would be tripping over all sorts of craziness, so we have to demonstrate to the Universe that we actually mean what we say. We need to take action to move ourselves towards that goal to show that we are serious about the goal.

We also need to be energetically in line with receiving the thing we are putting our attention on. Some things simply don't manifest instantly, nor should they, because we have to be ready. We have to be capable of receiving the things that we say we want. Most lottery winners lose everything within a few weeks or a few months, and that's because they don't have the energetic capacity for holding the amount of money they have just received overnight.

Also, remember that manifestation is not just about physical things.

We're just manifesting energy really. We can manifest the energy of love, or kindness or forgiveness. We can also manifest anger and arguments and stress and fear.

We can manifest healing. We can bring our bodies into a state of enormous health, or we can bring our bodies into a state of enormous unhealth. Think of the hypochondriacs you know. Think of the depressed people you know. I'm sorry depressed people I feel I can say these things because I've been a depressed person. A very depressed person. And I know that the more I focused on that depression and those awful heavy feelings, the harder it was to come out of them. Then those feelings would become even more dominant and it began to feel impossible to change anything.

Believe me when I say it does change. It can change little by gently turning the dial on things.

The problem is that, when we are depressed, we want to go from depressed to euphorically happy. Unfortunately, that is not going to happen. That is asking yourself to walk the entire length of the emotional scale. When we're in a neutral place, we don't sit thinking, oh my God I want to be happy, we just accept that we're in a neutral place. When we're in the extreme of depression or apathy, however, we look for the opposite extreme as if that's the thing that's going to change it.

All we need to do is simply take one small step up the emotional scale.

The emotional scale has been talked about extensively by a couple of authors (Abraham Hicks and David Hawkins, notably), so I'm not going to spend a lot of time talking about it. In summary, emotions have energy. The emotions at the lower end of the spectrum are things like depression, apathy and grief. These emotions have dense, heavy energies around them. It can be very difficult to move out of them. It's like being stuck in treacle.

When we begin to move up the emotional scale to emotions with higher vibrations like anger and courage, there is more freedom, more movement. It's a bit like going from ice to water to steam. The emotions with the highest vibrations are love, peace and joy.

When we're stuck in apathy and depression, joy and peace are a long way away. We need to move up the emotional scale bit by bit.

In summary, manifestation is a massively misunderstood thing. But believe me when I say you're manifesting every minute of every day.

Recently, I was on a Zoom call. There were seven of us and when we reached the last person to speak she said "I've got the gas man here and I bet he's going to need me now". He did !! She put that energy out into the Universe and the Universe obliged.

Careful what you wish for.

That expression has been around for a long time, for good reason. So do be careful what you wish for. Wish for what you truly desire, wish for what lights you up.

And remember, when you put your desires out, put the right energy into your requests. Let there be a lightness to your requests. Let them light up your heart. Matter coalesces around frequency so put the frequency out into the world that you are wanting to experience. Feel it with all five senses. Send it out on a high frequency. If your frequency is low, you will be given things to feel low about. When your frequency is high, you will be offered high-frequency results.

Sat Naam.

Chapter 11
Spirituality and Money

For this chapter, I'm going to take a little detour back into my personal experiences.

In my notes for writing this book, I have a little mind map, entitled *Breadcrumbs*. The reason for that is that when I look back over my own "spiritual awakening", I can see that there was a trail of metaphoric breadcrumbs, which has led me to where I am now.

I've written about many of these breadcrumbs as we've been going along, but it's the money piece that is where my passion lies. And it is the money piece which I have had to be my bravest self around. Money is such a touchy subject.

Once I had pitched myself in the lowest role I could find in my first corporate role in 20 years I, not surprisingly, found myself bored rigid. The first shock for me was walking into the office on my first day, and literally feeling like I had walked into a graveyard.

Now, don't get me wrong, that organisation was a lovely one with truly lovely people working there. But nobody spoke. When I left work to have my babies, the internet was just arriving in the workplace. We used to talk - on phones. We had fax machines whirring away in the background. This place I had walked into was so quiet. I was horrified.

That said, and looking at the positive, the silence offered me a great gift. Everybody was plugged into something on the internet, YouTube, Spotify and in my case, (and I have no idea how I came across it) an online summit called the Conscious Business Summit. Most of the speakers on this summit were North American apart from one quite posh English woman named **Sarah McCrum.** (https://www.thankyoumoney.com/courses/free-introductions?ref=18c579). Her voice engaged me instantly because it was English, and I was fascinated by her story and what she was saying. She and her then business partner, **Jeff Vander Clute**, (https://jeffvanderclute.com/) were discussing something called the Consciousness of Money.

Now, hang on a minute, they were describing money as living energy with intent. They were saying that they talked with money and that money was not just benign, it was benevolent and powerful and wanting to do good things in the world. They were saying that money is love.

This just sounded weird at the time. Surely money is the root of all evil. I had been told that it is easier for a camel to pass through the eye of a needle than it is for a rich man to get into heaven. Everyone assured me that money doesn't make you happy. I understood that if I have money someone else doesn't have money.

Could it really be true that money is a force for good? and that it wants to support people to do good work in the world? Could it really be true, that money is not a limited resource? and that we can choose how we spend and receive money? Could it be true that we can choose to move money on a current of love and light, rather than the more familiar currents of fear, shame and guilt? Could it be true that we can collectively make it be so?

I was hooked. These concepts were so different to anything I'd heard before. Sarah and Jeff were running online retreats around the consciousness of money and I signed up. [As I've said before, I always have enough money for any kind of spiritual or personal development].

I had to wake up at 2 o'clock in the morning to go to the sessions because Sarah was in Australia and Jeff was in America. This was my first experience of online training and, if I'm honest, being half asleep, I was probably not being my most conscious. But they had caught something inside me. My soul contract maybe. Whenever I have had a moment of wobble around my work and question what I'm doing invariably an alarm will go off, or some other thing will drop past me concerning money or abundance. I know that money is part of my spiritual journey and I am here to help others embrace its energy as love.

As the course came to an end, one of the other participants asked if any of us wanted to carry on working together. This exploration was so unconventional and she wanted to keep the momentum up.

Gradually, a small group of us formed. We are eight in total and have been meeting every Wednesday morning at 7am since April 2018. We've watched each other's ebbs and flows. We've witnessed growth and change, expansion and contraction, loss and gain, and shared the human experience with each other. We've grown close. Our exact line up has fluctuated a little over the years. And at the core of what we do is money.

Last year we got a little shakeup when our newest member, **Clare Chapman**, (https://www.consciousfinance.co.uk/) joined us. Clare is an accountant who described herself at the time as "an oil tanker becoming a dolphin". She brought more consciousness to our little tribe. We focused more on money as our core.

Clare is a great creator. She had a desire to go to Findhorn and she spoke it out loud to Jeff Vander Clute. Various elements lined up and Clare's intention became a reality. Her desire manifested and she has been living and working with the Findhorn Community for the best part of six months as I write.

Through her and her incredible manifestation, I was able to attend a workshop with Louis Bohtlingk in January of this year called Meeting the Mystery of Money (MMM). The weekend workshop is a shamanic journey, which takes the participants through a profound healing journey and integration of the energies around money.

Louis was gifted a download of a model of a Care First economy. In this model, care is what propels the economy and money follows. The MMM workshop was so profound for me (the name I adopted during the course of the workshop was Transformation) that it led me to create an online summit – (Healing) Money Talks - which aired in March. The summit is a series of 18 expansive conversations about money. These conversations do turn the conventional view and perception of money on its head. They makes space for us to view things differently and do things differently. The summit is still available to buy. And you can even choose the price point that best suits your budget. You can purchase it from the following link. https://healingmoney.kartra.com/page/healingmoneytalks

If you want to go deeper into your own personal money story, I have an eight-week online course that you can follow in your own time. This course is supported by a live Q&A every first Tuesday of the month.

Heal Your Money Wounds
https://healingmoney.kartra.com/page/healyourmoneywounds

And if you are running (or just starting out running) a heart centred business, I have new intakes for my Building Bountiful Businesses programme every month. The next intake begins on Thursday 1st July 2021.

This is a 90-day programme whose purpose is to support heart-centred business owners as they grow their businesses in a way that supports these concepts of money as love and guides us all out of this place of fear, not enough and lack.

Spaces on this course are strictly limited to a maximum of eight participants. If you are committed to making real shifts in your life and your business and are ready to invest the time and energy needed for these shifts to occur, you can find out more here. https://healingmoney.kartra.com/page/buildingbountifulbusinessesinfo

If you already know you want to be one of those eight you can see if you are a good fit for the course by scheduling a discovery call here. https://healingmoney.kartra.com/page/buildingbountifulbusinesses

My purpose in all my work is to help spiritual people to receive and welcome money into their lives and to support a new economy that is based on and created in love.

The most recent pieces of my puzzle are the work of **Peter Koenig** (https://peterkoenig.typepad.com/eng/) and my work with Buddy and David on Silence With.

In both cases, these projects are creating a currency out of doing the things we love – literally creating money from love.

Just imagine, money created in love. Money moving on lines of love, being spent with love, being received with love. No more fear, no more scarcity. There is plenty to go around. Lack is a myth. Remember that vegetable patch. Remember your programming. A spiritual awakening is changing the hard drive.

A few quick points about money and practices which can really ease your energy around it.

- Be grateful for all the money you have received and continue to receive in your life.

- Focus on what comes in. Remember. Energy flows where focus goes.

- Bless all the money that comes in and out of your life, I mean that. As you tap your card or hand over notes, literally thank the money, bless it. The Japanese word for thank you is Arigato. This word means much more than just thank you. It has depth and reverence. As you pay silently vibrate the expression Arigato.

- Bring consciousness to your financial transactions. Be aware of what you're doing. Don't just spend money like it's going out of fashion. Spend money in a way that you're aware of what you're doing.

- Treat money as you would your beloved:
    - Notice it.
    - Appreciate it.
    - Love it. It loves you.
    - Treat it kindly and with respect
        - Keep your purse/wallet tidy
        - Check your bank and credit card statements

Finally, drop the fear around money.

Sat Naam

Chapter 12
Going Forward

This is the last chapter of the book, and it's going to be short. The title of the book, as you know, is:

What The F**k Is A Spiritual Awakening, Anyway?

You're having a spiritual awakening. You wouldn't be reading this book if you weren't, [unless of course you're one of my relatives and doing so under duress !!].

If I may, I will give you my top takeaways from my own experience.

The **number one** thing to do is to open yourself up to the possibility that there is more going on the planet than meets the eyes, the nose, the ears, the skin and the tongue.

Number two on my list is to create a meditation practice.

Number three - make space for "spirit" (however you define it) to reveal itself to you and listen to what it is saying.

Number four - follow the breadcrumbs. Your trail will be different to mine. Maybe this book is your first breadcrumb. Maybe it is your 100th breadcrumb. It doesn't matter either way. Recognise that it is one and be open to what will come out of reading it.

Number five -be careful what you wish for. And track what you get. If you talk about arguing with your partner, you're pretty much guaranteed to get an argument with your partner. Always remember that words (and their energy) make worlds. If you spend your time - like I did for too many years - grumbling to yourself about how miserable you are, guess what ...

Number six - release your past. Your life today is an exact representation of what you have manifested to date. Today is the first day of the rest of your life, take these steps and start creating something different.

Number seven - let go of emotions that don't serve you. I strongly recommend you read Letting Go by David Hawkins. It is quite a weighty tome. Ask And It Is Given by Abraham Hicks is a little lighter. The message in both of these books is to not hang on to emotions – especially those with lower vibrations. Simply let them pass through you. They will come and they will go. Remember, this too will pass.

Number eight - surround yourself with like-hearted people. It can be a lonely journey, talking about things and experiencing things that 90% of the population simply don't understand and are not experiencing. It really does help to be in the company of other people who understand you and speak the same language.

Number nine - be grateful for everything you have received to date, everything you have in this present moment and everything that is still to come. Gratitude, to me, is the most important point on the list.

Mountains of books have been written about gratitude. Create a daily gratitude practice - ideally, be consciously grateful at least twice a day. I recommend topping and tailing your day with gratitude. Before you know it, you will be looking for things to be grateful for and you will find them. Go on a 28-day rampage of gratitude. Buy The Magic by Rhonda Byrne and do the practices.

Number 10 - love. Remember Jesus' messages about the heart. Trust your heart. Breathe, often into your heart space. Be open to what your heart is telling you.

Finally **number 11** - trust and believe. You're not going mad. This really is happening. Follow your instincts. Follow the breadcrumbs. If you feel called to follow any of the links in this book, do it. You won't regret it. That is your intuition, telling you that you need more of this. We're a lovely bunch us spiritual types and we can't wait to welcome you.

About the Author

Emma Lucy Wall is a teacher, a healer, a coach and mentor. She is a trained Kundalini Yoga teacher, a natural tantrica, a rapid results business coach and Instant Miracle healer.

Emma uses her eclectic skills and training to provide support to heart-centred business owners who are tired of the old programming and ready to step into the most expanded version of themselves.

With a passion for healing the energy around money, Emma likes to be known as

The Tantric Money Healer

She draws upon a wide variety of disciplines to create her own unique style of teaching and coaching.

At the heart of everything Emma teaches is energy.

Energy is everywhere and in everything. It is the pulsing beat of the entire Universe.

When you know how to train it you can quite literally create anything in your life.

Through an incredible tool kit of tried and tested techniques and teachings, Emma shows her clients the steps they need to take to become the fullest expression of themselves in this lifetime.

She works with people who are ready to step bravely into the next chapter and do the work necessary to be the change they want to be in their lives and the world.

If there is a bigger you waiting to be uncovered, you can reach out to Emma via email – emma@raisingkundalini.co.uk

You can see her in action on her YouTube channel.
https://www.youtube.com/channel/UCHR5KoqZjpyEvRpdkam1l6g
Emma is a trailblazer and is joyfully moving away from the old social media channels.

You can follow her on Clubhouse (@tantricmoney) where she loves to join and moderate rooms.

She would love you to join her there and share your energy. Come as you are and prepare to grow.

Other Books and Services by the Author

Emma has already started work on her next book Demystifying The Money Game.

You can find out about Emma's services and how to work with her by visiting her website.

https://emmalucywall.com

Emma offers one-to-one and group business coaching and mentoring.

Her speciality is supporting wise, heart-centred businesses women to heal their relationships with money in order to grow their business in a way that feels aligned to their core values.

She loves to help her clients weave spirituality into their working lives and to harness the powers of the Universe to make a real difference in the world.

Products

(Healing) Money Talks
https://healingmoney.kartra.com/page/healingmoneytalks
A series of 18 conversations concerned with shifting the energies around money from fear to love

Heal Your Money Wounds
https://healingmoney.kartra.com/page/healyourmoneywounds
An eight week online self study programme supported by live Q&As every first Tuesday of the month

Building Bountiful Businesses
https://healingmoney.kartra.com/page/buildingbountifulbusinessesinfo
A 90 day programme for heart-centred wise women business owners who are ready to up-level their businesses

YouTube Channel
https://www.youtube.com/channel/UCHR5KoqZjpyEvRpdkam1l6g

One More Thing Before You Go…

If you enjoyed reading this book or found it useful, I'd be very grateful if you'd post a short review on Amazon.
Your support really does make a difference, and I read all the reviews personally, so I can get your feedback and make this book even better.

If you would like to leave a review, then all you need to do is click the review link on Amazon here:
You will be shown how to get your review links to place here.

And if you live in the UK, you can leave it here:
You will be shown how to get your review links to place here.

Thanks again for your support!

Printed in Great Britain
by Amazon